THE FAST TRACK

Biblical Fasting that Produces Rapid Results

SAM O. ADEWUNMI

COVENANT PUBLISHING

The Fast track: Biblical Fasting that Produces Rapid Results
Sam O. Adewunmi

Unless otherwise stated, all scripture quotations are taken from the Holy Bible, King James Version (NKJV). Other versions cited are NIV, KJV, GNB and AMP.

ISBN 978-1-907734-18-2

First Edition
First Printing January 2017

No part of this publication may be produced, distorted or transmitted in any form or by any means, including photocopying, recording or other electronic or mechanical methods, without the prior written permission of the publisher, or except in the case of brief quotations embodied in critical reviews and certain other noncommercial uses permitted by copyright law.

For permission requests, write to the publisher, addressed "Attention: Permission Coordinator" at the email address below:

Covenant Publishing
samadewunmi@btinternet.com

Covenant Publishing is part of New Covenant Church
Charity Registered in England & Wales number 1004343
Registered Address: 506-510 Old Kent Road. LONDON SE1 5BA

Copyright © January 2017, Sam O. Adewunmi
All rights reserved

Cover Design by Covenant Publishing Team
Published by Covenant Publishing
Photography by David Adetoye
Printed in the United Kingdom

TABLE OF CONTENT

Dedication	v
Introduction – The Importance of Fasting	7

Chapters

1	The Actual Meaning of Fasting	17
2	Fasting in the Old Testament	23
3	Types of Fasts	47
4	Duration of Fasts	55
5	Jesus' Teaching on Fasting	65
6	Fasting in the New Testament	75
7	Fasting for Power	87
8	The Shallow Fast	101
9	Acceptable Fast	113
10	Benefits of Acceptable Fast	129
11	The Daniel Fast	137
12	Why all Major Religion Fast	147
13	Fasting Prayer Points with Scriptures	157

DEDICATION

To my parents Chief Olufemi Adewunmi and Chief (Mrs) Felicia Adewunmi (both of blessed memories) for showing me the way of the Lord.

INTRODUCTION

THE IMPORTANCE OF FASTING

"Some have exalted religious fasting beyond all Scripture and reason, and others have utterly disregarded it." - JOHN WESLEY

A lot of Christians think fasting belong to the Old Covenant, and so neglect the practice. They do not see the need for or the benefit of a Christian fast. The assumption is that faith and belief are sufficient to get things done. Thus fasting is confined to the occasional once-a-year Lenten or the when-I-feel-like practice. "It has no value, and I just cannot be bothered," some say. From the middle of the nineteenth century to the midst of the twentieth century, there was little or no mention of fasting among some brethren. That is almost a century of relegating the spiritual discipline of fast.

Those of the other opinion, who say that you must fast for nearly all reason, also would claim that you cannot live a successful Christian life for a whole week without fasting. They do it habitually without being able to justify their practice. They tie holiness and righteous living to fasting. They live an ascetic lifestyle of barely eating half of the year; fasting for days and months unending.

Why is this contradiction? What is causing the confusion? Who is right?

There is a mystery surrounding fasting. This is why all religion fasts. The Protestants (Mainline and Evangelicals), the Pagan, the Bahá'í, the Buddhist, the Hindu, the Catholics, the Eastern Orthodox, the Mormons, the Jews, and the Muslim; they all fast.

Notable persons in the Bible also fasted; Moses the lawgiver, David the king, Elijah the prophet, Esther the queen, Daniel, the seer, Jesus the Messiah, Paul, the apostle, and other Apostles.

None Christians in the New Testament were also recorded to have fasted; Anna the prophet, Saul the persecutor, and Cornelius the devout.

In the pages of the New Testament, you will find that there is more teaching on fasting than

Introduction

on repentance and confession! Jesus taught more on fasting than He did in His teachings on baptism and the Lord's Supper!

With such interest placed on fasting by most faiths, the Christians and none Christians alike, to disregard the importance of fasting may be detrimental to your Christian experience and to exalt the practice beyond worth may equally be unfruitful.

As the Bible has so much to reveal on the subject of fasting, considering what it says is only right.

THE DREAM TEAM

Luke's gospel reveal a link between prayer and fasting.

> "And this woman was a widow of about eighty-four years, who did not depart from the temple, but served God with fastings and prayers night and day" (Luke 2:37).

> "Then they said to Him, "Why do the disciples of John fast often and make prayers, and likewise those of the

Pharisees, but Yours eat and drink?" (Luke 5:33).

Prayer, faith (believing), and confession are great tools of power ministry. However, there is a level of power ministry that those three cannot scale. According to Jesus, there are times when faith and confession are not enough. At these times, prayer and confession joined with fasting is necessary. Fasting joined with prayer and confession will accomplish things which normal faith may not.

> *"So Jesus said to them, "Because of your unbelief; for assuredly, I say to you, if you have faith as a mustard seed, you will say to this mountain, 'Move from here to there,' and it will move; and nothing will be impossible for you. However, this kind does not go out except by prayer and fasting" (Matthew 17:20-21).*
>
> *"So He said to them, "This kind can come out by nothing but prayer and fasting" (Mark 9:29).*

Jesus mentioned words like 'unbelief,' 'say' (which is confession), and 'faith' as ingredients of power ministry. However, He concluded that there is a higher level of operation that demands the combined tools of prayer and fasting.

In other words, some demonic problems can only be solved when you fast, though you may still be able to achieve a level of success without fasting.

The scriptures above conclusively stated the necessity of combining prayer and fasting when faced with demons of epilepsy (or the deaf and dumb spirit).

BREAKING SATANIC STRONGHOLD

As Adam and Eve fell through eating, we can also conquer through fasting. A very direct way of attacking the devil is to show your devotion to God by denying your flesh of whatever food it needs. If the devil cannot use food to tempt you, he has lost control over your life. Fasting, therefore, becomes a tool to fight the flesh and the devil. It is a very potent weapon of both attack and defence you can unleash on the enemy of your soul.

Food is always an area the devil will tempt you. He did that to Jesus. It was not surprising that the devil tempted Him in three points; the lust of the flesh (eating), the lust of the eyes and the pride of life. To achieve maximum impact,

Jesus was asked to turn stones into bread (food), jump from a mountain top, and bow down to Satan. However, Jesus did not fall for any of the devil's deceit.

In other to accomplish complete takeover from Satan, Jesus had to refuse the food offered Him by the devil.

FASTING IS SACRIFICIAL

Most sacrifices performed under the Old Covenant required the burning of the fat. To appease God, the blood of the sacrifice and the fat were forbidden to be eaten by anyone. The fat belonged to God.

> *"And the priest shall sprinkle the blood on the altar of the Lord at the door of the tabernacle of meeting, and burn the fat for a sweet aroma to the Lord" (Leviticus 17:6).*

> *"And the priest shall burn them on the altar as food, an offering made by fire for a sweet aroma; all the fat is the Lord's. 'This shall be a perpetual statute throughout your generations in all your dwellings:*

Introduction

you shall eat neither fat nor blood'"
(Leviticus 3:16-17).

It is a known scientific and medical fact that once the body had used up its reserves of glucose, it burns fat for energy. So when we fast, we are burning fat as a sacrifice unto God. Like me, if you have fasted before, we become so frail, fragile and feeble, especially with our knees. This is awesome; we truly have become the sacrificial lambs. Fasting is powerful, glory to God.

"My knees are weak through fasting, and my flesh is feeble from lack of fatness"
(Psalms 109:24).

THE FAST TRACK

When meditating on the right title for this book, two came to mind – the fast lane and the fast track. One is focused on the right way of fasting, and the other is focused on the fastest way of fasting. Which then is considered appropriate? As a noun, fast track is a route or method which provides for more rapid results than usual. As a verb, it means to accelerate the progress of a person or project.

THE FAST TRACK

The fast track talks about speed. The fast lane, however, describes a lane of a motorway or dual carriageway for use by traffic that is overtaking or moving more quickly than the rest. Though they look similar, you may have to change your route with the fast track, but with the fast lane, only a shift in lane is required. Most of what you would read would explore the two options.

I chose the fast track simply because I wanted you to consider a paradigm shift; a change in your thinking when you ponder fasting. I had you in mind. I wanted you to get the right result and not just do the right things. I wanted your fasting experience to be both effective and efficient.

I have looked at every single scripture in the bible on fasting, studying the purposes, the principles and the practices of each.

Please approach this book with care; it may affect you. If you are the religious type, please don't hate me. I beg of you not to throw away the freedom from religious spirit you have been craving. There are things I have addressed in the book that your church or denomination may disagree with. For me, it was not easy to let go of this stuff I have held onto for close to five decades. However, God had to deal with me

Introduction

before I started writing. I have had to learn and unlearned several things in the process of studying the subject.

If you read this book with an open mind, three things will happen; you will regain your freedom from religious fast by the time you finish, you will become more successful and fulfilled when you fast the right way, and above all, you will get better results quicker. I know that is what you want. So let's go digging.

THE FAST TRACK

CHAPTER 1

THE ACTUAL MEANING OF FASTING

Biblical fasting is going without food. The noun translated "fast" or "a fasting" is *'tsom'* in the Hebrew and *'nesteia'* in the Greek language. It means the voluntary abstinence from food. The literal Hebrew translation would be "not to eat." The literal Greek says "no food."

Unger's Bible Dictionary explains that the word fast in the Bible is the Hebrew word *'sum,'* meaning, "to cover" the mouth, or from the Greek word *'nesteuo,'* meaning "to abstain." For spiritual purposes, it means to go without eating and drinking.

> ""*Go, gather all the Jews who are present in Shushan, and fast for me; neither eat nor drink for three days, night or day. My maids and I will fast likewise. And so I*

will go to the king, which is against the law; and if I perish, I perish!"" (Esther 4:16).

If fasting directly relates to not eating food, it suffices to say that any other fasting outside abstinence from food is unacceptable. Many people have recommended a fast from sex, cigarettes, television, the internet, social media, and so on, as equal in significance to not eating food. Some have even suggested that those on medication or unable to fast due to medical reasons or being pregnant can abstain from other things in other to make up for their inability to fast. It is claimed that the same mission can be accomplished whether it is a fast from food or other things considered significant.

While I understand the need to be sensitive to people who may not be able to fast yet are desiring the same results that fasting produces, nowhere in scripture was fasting anything other than abstinence from food or drink. Apart from Christianity, no other religion has ever permitted this trade-off when it comes to the subject of fasting.

Cutting off certain activities in other to focus our attention on God is a form of self-denial, but it does not have and cannot produce the same

Chapter 1 – The Actual Meaning of Fasting

effect as fasting from food. When you fast from food, it will have a noticeable effect on your body putting it under 'subjection' and weakening the devil's stronghold on your appetite.

This crystallises the fact that fasting is to deny the body of food. If you choose to fast, it is an exercise that will put you in charge of your body and help you to sharpen your physical Saw, so you can become more effective for God. Fasting this way allows you to align your spirit with the Spirit of God so that His ability can be transferred to your inability and His Omnipotence can overshadow your impotence.

> *"But those who wait for the Lord [who expect, look for, and hope in Him] shall change and renew their strength and power; they shall lift their wings and mount up [close to God] as eagles [mount up to the sun]; they shall run and not be weary, they shall walk and not faint or become tired" (Isaiah 40:31 AMP).*

THE FAST TRACK

THE ONLY FAST

Although other national fast days are mentioned in the Bible, The Day of Atonement is the only fast day commanded by God.

> *"And the LORD spoke to Moses, saying: "Also the tenth day of this seventh month shall be the Day of Atonement. It shall be a holy convocation for you; you shall afflict your souls, and offer an offering made by fire to the LORD. And you shall do no work on that same day, for it is the Day of Atonement, to make atonement for you before the LORD your God. For any person who is not afflicted in soul on that same day shall be cut off from his people. And anyone who does any work on that same day, that person I will destroy from among his people. You shall do no manner of work; it shall be a statute forever throughout your generations in all your dwellings. It shall be to you a Sabbath of solemn rest, and you shall afflict your souls; on the ninth day of the month at evening, from evening to evening, you shall celebrate your Sabbath"" (Leviticus 23:26-32).*

Chapter 1 – The Actual Meaning of Fasting

> *"'On the tenth day of this seventh month, you shall have a holy convocation. You shall afflict your souls; you shall not do any work"* (Numbers 29:7).

Though not called "fasting," the phrase "afflicting one's soul" was understood to refer to fasting. The Psalmist said,

> *"When I wept and chastened my soul with fasting, that became my reproach"* (Psalms 69:10).

When Jesus taught about fasting, He regarded fasting as mourning. Mourning here is the same as afflicting the soul.

> *"Then the disciples of John came to Him, saying, "Why do we and the Pharisees fast often, but Your disciples do not fast? And Jesus said to them, "Can the friends of the bridegroom mourn as long as the bridegroom is with them? But the days will come when the bridegroom will be taken away from them, and then they will fast"* (Matthew 9:14-15).

Also in Acts, Apostle Paul described the term 'Fast' as the Day of Atonement.

> *"Now when much time had been spent, and sailing was now dangerous because the Fast was already over, Paul advised them"* *(Acts 27:9).*

Let us now look at the other fasts in the Old Testament so as to glean some understanding about Old Covenant fasting.

CHAPTER 2

FASTING IN THE OLD TESTAMENT

As we go through the Old Testament scriptures, we would discover that the people of God fasted for various reasons and different patterns. There is a lot to learn from their fasts.

FASTING FOR MERCY

In 2 Samuel 12, the story is told that King David fathered a child from his adulterous relationship with Bathsheba, Uriah's wife. We read that the child became ill soon after he was born. In repentance for his iniquity and intercession for the life of the innocent child, David sought the pardon of God through the avenue of fasting. Without ever knowing if God was going to be merciful and without any indication of how long it might take before God would answer, he went into isolation and seclusion and refused to eat. Now let's read what followed,

> *"Then Nathan went home. The Lord caused the child that Uriah's wife had borne to David to become very ill. David prayed to God that the child would get well. He refused to eat anything, and every night he went into his room and spent the night lying on the floor. His court officials went to him and tried to make him get up, but he refused and would not eat anything with them. A week later the child died, and David's officials were afraid to tell him the news. They said, "While the child was living, David wouldn't answer us when we spoke to him. How can we tell him that his child is dead? He might do himself some harm!" When David noticed them whispering to each other, he realised that the child had died. So he asked them, "Is the child dead?" "Yes, he is," they answered. David got up from the floor, had a bath, combed his hair, and changed his clothes. Then he went and worshipped in the house of the Lord. When he*

Chapter 2 – Fasting in the Old Testament

returned to the palace, he asked for food and ate it as soon as it was served. "We don't understand this," his officials said to him. "While the child was alive, you wept for him and would not eat; but as soon as he died, you got up and ate!" "Yes," David answered, "I did fast and weep while he was still alive. I thought that the Lord might be merciful to me and not let the child die. But now that he is dead, why should I fast? Could I bring the child back to life? I will someday go to where he is, but he can never come back to me"" (2 Samuel 12:15-23 GNB).

Here, the GNB used the word 'merciful,' but in the KJV and in the NKJV, it was translated as 'gracious.'

Let's observe here; seeking God's mercy through prayer and fasting cannot be scheduled for a set period. It may take as short as one day or as long as forty-one days. David got a reply on the seventh day.

Also, the fact that our reply did not meet our request or expectations is not indicative of a withheld pardon. Earlier, when confronted by Prophet Nathan because of his sin, David repented and was granted a pardon.

THE FAST TRACK

"So David said to Nathan, "I have sinned against the LORD." And Nathan said to David, "The LORD also has put away your sin; you shall not die" (2 Samuel 12:13).

But why? Why do we ask God for mercy, especially for an innocent child, and we receive a 'no' answer. Well, I have no clue. All we care to know is that God is omniscient. In David's case, had the child's life been spared, there could have been a few negative outcomes or reactions. He could have had a terrible life and faced rejection by the community that he could have taken his own life. Who knows?

"... And he moved on." The Bible says,

"David got up from the floor, had a bath, combed his hair, and changed his clothes. Then he went and worshipped in the house of the Lord. When he returned to the palace, he asked for food and ate it as soon as it was served" (2 Samuel 12:20 GNB).

After you have fasted and sought the face of God to receive mercy if the outcomes seem undesirable, do not get stuck; move on. Don't allow your sins of your past to hold you back.

Chapter 2 – Fasting in the Old Testament

You have done the best right thing, now do the next best thing; move on. The NLT says, David 'put on lotions.' Get you some perfume and wear a good smell.

The last point I would like to make on David's story is one that challenges even the most matured believer. Perhaps, a lesson that no one would ever be too matured to learn. David worshiped God; even after his plea for mercy was refused. Worship? Yes, worship. That is right.

> *"David got up from the floor, had a bath, combed his hair, and changed his clothes. Then he went and worshipped in the house of the Lord. When he returned to the palace, he asked for food and ate it as soon as it was served"* (2 Samuel 12:20 GNB).

Don't blame God if He decides to exercise His sovereignty and refuses your request following a fast. Just like David, let God be God and accept His decision.

THE FAST TRACK

FASTING FOR OTHER PEOPLE'S WELLBEING

There is at least one instance in the Bible where we read that it was acceptable to intercede for someone in prayer, with or without their knowledge or consent, so that their situation might be improved. It suggests that God will hear us when we pray for them to be blessed, healed and delivered.

Intercessory prayer on behalf of someone has always been a major theme in Scripture but what is unusual is the place of fasting in the scheme of prayer intervention.

More so, how could someone even consider praying for their enemies let alone fasting as well. That was David's decision when his arch rivals were sick. He fasted for the wellbeing of his enemies even when they were unaware he was doing so. His strategy to get his enemies to back off was to pray for their healing. He was sure that if all were well with them, they would cease to trouble him.

The lesson here is not that they were healed but that it is right for us as believers to intercede for someone even if they are unaware or have not requested us to do so. It makes us liberated.

Chapter 2 – Fasting in the Old Testament

"But as for me, when they were sick, My clothing was sackcloth; I humbled myself with fasting; And my prayer would return to my own heart" (Psalm 35:13).

PROTECTION AGAINST A MORE POWERFUL ENEMY

There is a well-documented story in 2 Chronicles 20 of three powerful nations gathered in battle array against the people of God. King Jehoshaphat heard that the Moabites, Ammonites and the people of Mount Seir wanted to attack Israel. Learning of the plot, he decided to seek God and proclaimed a fast throughout all Judah. The fast only lasted a single day, but its effects were amazing, and the gathering of the spoil of victory lasted three days. Here is the sequence of the story and the lessons learnt:

Day 1
- Plot revealed (verses 1-2)
- Fast proclaimed (verses 3-4)
- Prayers offered (verses 5-13)
- Prophecy received (verses 14-17) and
- Praises raised (verses 18-19)

Day 2
- Praises raised (verses 20-21)
- Army took position (verses 20-21)
- Enemies destroyed each other (verses 22-24)

Days 2-4: Gathering of the spoil (verse 25)

Day 4: Return with victory praise (verses 26-28)

There are three key elements to this story: fasting, praying and praising. When we humble ourselves before His Majesty, He will turn our enemies against each other. The victory was one of self-destruction.

After the people had fasted, God revealed the battle strategy and the people praise Him. The fast stirred up the spirit of prophecy and the revelation that brought victory.

Just one more thing. The people praised God; before the victory, during the battle, and after. The whole encounter was wrapped up in praise. People today praise God after the victory.

In another incident, Ezra led the Babylonian captives through a dangerous road back to Jerusalem. They had to pass through enemy territories unarmed and unprotected. Therefore

Chapter 2 – Fasting in the Old Testament

their only covering was God, the help of Whom they sought through fasting.

> *"Then I proclaimed a fast there at the river of Ahava, that we might humble ourselves before our God, to seek from Him the right way for us and our little ones and all our possessions." "For I was ashamed to request of the king an escort of soldiers and horsemen to help us against the enemy on the road, because we had spoken to the king, saying, "The hand of our God is upon all those for good who seek Him, but His power and His wrath are against all those who forsake Him." So we fasted and entreated our God for this, and He answered our prayer" (Ezra 8:21-23).*

> *"Then we departed from the river of Ahava on the twelfth day of the first month, to go to Jerusalem. And the hand of our God was upon us, and He delivered us from the hand of the enemy and from ambush along the road" (Ezra 8:31).*

THE FAST TRACK

FASTING WHEN FACED WITH IMPENDING DANGER

Do you want to see God move on your behalf so you can achieve the impossible? Then fast and seek His help. Queen Esther commanded the Jews living in Shushan to join her in fasting to seek God's help before approaching King Nebuchadnezzar for a dangerous request. At the time, the Jews were already fasting for their lives but now had to fast for Esther's safety as well.

> *"And in every province where the king's command and decree arrived, there was great mourning among the Jews, with fasting, weeping, and wailing; and many lay in sackcloth and ashes. Go, gather all the Jews who are present in Shushan, and fast for me; neither eat nor drink for three days, night or day. My maids and I will fast likewise. And so I will go to the king, which is against the law; and if I perish, I perish!"" (Esther 4:3, 16).*

> *"Now it happened on the third day that Esther put on her royal robes and stood in the inner court of the king's palace, across from the king's house, while the king sat*

Chapter 2 – Fasting in the Old Testament

> *on his royal throne in the royal house, facing the entrance of the house. So it was, when the king saw Queen Esther standing in the court, that she found favor in his sight, and the king held out to Esther the golden scepter that was in his hand. Then Esther went near and touched the top of the scepter. And the king said to her, "What do you wish, Queen Esther? What is your request? It shall be given to you - up to half the kingdom!"" (Esther 5:1-3).*

The same strategy was adopted by Nehemiah in the book that bears his name. Like Esther, Nehemiah took a significant risk in seeking the help of King Artaxerxes so he could rebuild the walls of Jerusalem. As the cupbearer to the King, he was always expected to be happy and cheerful. Knowing it would be a dangerous move, seeking God's help first with prayer and fasting was inevitable. The book recorded that he got the help he needed.

> *"So it was, when I heard these words, that I sat down and wept, and mourned for many days; I was fasting and praying before the God of heaven" (Nehemiah 1:4).*

THE FAST TRACK

"And it came to pass in the month of Nisan, in the twentieth year of King Artaxerxes, when wine was before him, that I took the wine and gave it to the king. Now I had never been sad in his presence before. Therefore the king said to me, "Why is your face sad, since you are not sick? This is nothing but sorrow of heart." So I became dreadfully afraid, and said to the king, "May the king live forever! Why should my face not be sad, when the city, the place of my fathers' tombs, lies waste, and its gates are burned with fire?" Then the king said to me, "What do you request?" So I prayed to the God of heaven" (Nehemiah 2:1-4).

In the same manner, Ezra fasted for the lives of the Jews that had been taken captive.

"Then Ezra rose up from before the house of God, and went into the chamber of Johanan the son of Eliashib: and [when] he came thither, he did eat no bread, nor drink water: for he mourned because of the transgression of them that had been carried away" (Ezra 10:6 KJV).

Chapter 2 – Fasting in the Old Testament

FASTING TO INQUIRE OF THE LORD

When the whole of Israel was set in battle array against the Benjamites, they asked God which tribe to go first, and God answered back that they should send Judah. They were defeated. Twenty-two thousand of them were killed. So they went to inquire of God what to do. This time, they were assured victory. They lost the battle again, and eighteen thousand people died.

The Israelites a third time, went to inquire of the Lord what to do, but this time, they fasted from morning to evening. God not only gave assurance of victory but the timing as well. When we inquire of the Lord with fasting, it is a demonstration of our seriousness on the matter.

> *"Then all the Israelites, the whole army, went up to Bethel, and there they sat weeping before the Lord. They fasted that day until evening and presented burnt offerings and fellowship offerings to the Lord. And the Israelites inquired of the Lord. (In those days the ark of the covenant of God was there, with Phinehas son of Eleazar, the son of Aaron, ministering before it.) They asked, "Shall*

we go up again to fight against the Benjamites, our fellow Israelites, or not?" The Lord responded, "Go, for tomorrow I will give them into your hands"" (Judges 20:26-28 NIV).

FASTING FOR REPENTANCE AND REDEDICATION

There was once a time that the Philistines fought against Israel, defeated Israel, captured the ark of God, killing Eli's two sons, Hophni and Phinehas in the process. The Israelites knew their defeat was a result of their sin of serving foreign gods. They became subjects to the Philistines for seven months before they were able to defeat them. Before they could face the Philistines in battle again, they had to fast.

"Then Samuel said, "Assemble all Israel at Mizpah, and I will intercede with the Lord for you." When they had assembled at Mizpah, they drew water and poured it out before the Lord. On that day they fasted and there they confessed, "We have sinned against the Lord." Now Samuel was serving as leader of Israel at Mizpah. So the Philistines were subdued, and they

Chapter 2 – Fasting in the Old Testament

stopped invading Israel's territory. Throughout Samuel's lifetime, the hand of the Lord was against the Philistines" (1 Samuel 7:5-6, 13 NIV).

In a case similar to this, the entire people of Israel separated themselves to fast for repentance for ignoring and disobeying God. So it is perfect to return to God after a period of separation from Him and His will, fasting for even just a day as the Israelites did.

"Now on the twenty-fourth day of this month, the children of Israel were assembled with fasting, in sackcloth, and with dust on their heads. Then those of Israelite lineage separated themselves from all foreigners, and they stood and confessed their sins and the iniquities of their fathers. And they stood up in their place and read from the Book of the Law of the Lord their God for one-fourth of the day; and for another fourth they confessed and worshiped the Lord their God" (Nehemiah 9:1-3).

THE FAST TRACK

FASTING TO AVERT THE WRATH OF GOD

When God was going to kill King Ahab for supporting Jezebel his wife in the murder of Naboth, and for following after strange gods, Ahab decided to humble himself with fasting and God changed His mind.

> *"But there was no one like Ahab who sold himself to do wickedness in the sight of the LORD because Jezebel his wife stirred him up. And he behaved very abominably in following idols, according to all that the Amorites had done, whom the LORD had cast out before the children of Israel. So it was, when Ahab heard those words, that he tore his clothes and put sackcloth on his body, and fasted and lay in sackcloth, and went about mourning. And the word of the LORD came to Elijah the Tishbite, saying, "See how Ahab has humbled himself before Me? Because he has humbled himself before Me, I will not bring the calamity in his days. In the days of his son, I will bring the calamity on his house""* (1 Kings 21:25-29).

Chapter 2 – Fasting in the Old Testament

TURNING AWAY GOD'S JUDGEMENT

When the people of Nineveh cried out to God in fasting and repentance, God changed His mind and did not destroy them as previously planned.

> *"And Jonah began to enter the city on the first day's walk. Then he cried out and said, "Yet forty days and Nineveh shall be overthrown!" So the people of Nineveh believed God, proclaimed a fast, and put on sackcloth, from the greatest to the least of them. Who can tell if God will turn and relent, and turn away from His fierce anger, so that we may not perish? Then God saw their works, that they turned from their evil way; and God relented from the disaster that He had said He would bring upon them, and He did not do it" (Jonah 3:4-5, 9-10).*

In intercessory prayers, it is legitimate for someone to stand in the gap and asked God to pardon the sins of another, more so if the intercessor is a spiritual leader or a servant of God. Moses and Daniel stood in the gap in repentance for the sins of Israel.

THE FAST TRACK

""So I turned and came down from the mountain, and the mountain burned with fire, and the two tablets of the covenant were in my two hands. And I looked, and behold, you had sinned against the LORD your God—had made for yourselves a molded calf! You had turned aside quickly from the way which the LORD had commanded you. Then I took the two tablets and threw them out of my two hands and broke them before your eyes. And I fell down before the LORD, as at the first, forty days and forty nights; I neither ate bread nor drank water, because of all your sin which you committed in doing wickedly in the sight of the LORD, to provoke Him to anger" (Deuteronomy 9:15-18).

"Then I set my face toward the Lord God to make request by prayer and supplications, with fasting, sackcloth, and ashes. And I prayed to the LORD my God, and made confession, and said, "O Lord, great and awesome God, who keeps His covenant and mercy with those who love Him, and with those who keep His commandments, we have sinned and

Chapter 2 – Fasting in the Old Testament

committed iniquity, we have done wickedly and rebelled, even by departing from Your precepts and Your judgments" (Daniel 9:3-5).

RESTORATION OF GLORY

If you have been wrongfully imprisoned or your glory has been destroyed, the exercise of fasting and praying with genuine repentance will restore your glory and set you free. The book of Joel shows that God will hear and restore His people back to their former glory if they seek Him with fasting. The captives of Judah and Jerusalem were brought back, and their captors were judged.

> *"Consecrate a fast, Call a sacred assembly; Gather the elders And all the inhabitants of the land Into the house of the LORD your God, And cry out to the LORD"* (Joel 1:14).

> *""Now, therefore," says the LORD, "Turn to Me with all your heart, With fasting, with weeping, and with mourning." So rend your heart, and not your garments; Return to the LORD your*

THE FAST TRACK

God, For He is gracious and merciful, Slow to anger, and of great kindness; And He relents from doing harm. Who knows if He will turn and relent, And leave a blessing behind Him— A grain offering and a drink offering For the LORD your God? Blow the trumpet in Zion, Consecrate a fast, Call a sacred assembly; Gather the people, Sanctify the congregation, Assemble the elders, Gather the children and nursing babes; Let the bridegroom go out from his chamber, And the bride from her dressing room. Let the priests, who minister to the LORD, Weep between the porch and the altar; Let them say, "Spare Your people, O LORD, And do not give Your heritage to reproach, That the nations should rule over them. Why should they say among the peoples, 'Where is their God?' "" (Joel 2:12-17).

"And it will come to pass in that day That the mountains shall drip with new wine, the hills shall flow with milk, and all the brooks of Judah shall be flooded with water; A fountain shall flow from the house of the LORD And water the Valley of Acacias. "Egypt shall be a desolation,

Chapter 2 – Fasting in the Old Testament

and Edom a desolate wilderness, because of violence against the people of Judah, for they have shed innocent blood in their land. But Judah shall abide forever, And Jerusalem from generation to generation. For I will acquit them of the guilt of bloodshed, whom I had not acquitted; For the LORD dwells in Zion"" (Joel 3:18-21).

MOURNING THE DEATH OF A LOVED ONE

Under the Old Covenant, the death of someone dear is mourned by the community with some form of fasting. This was a natural reaction to grief over their loss.

Two examples come to mind. First, the men of Jabesh-Gilead mourned King Paul's death with a seven-day fast. The second was the same incident where David mourned with fasting until evening when he heard that Jonathan his friend had been killed alongside his father.

"Now when the inhabitants of Jabesh Gilead heard what the Philistines had done to Saul, all the valiant men arose and traveled all night, and took the body of Saul and the bodies of his sons from the

wall of Beth Shan; and they came to Jabesh and burned them there. Then they took their bones and buried them under the tamarisk tree at Jabesh, and fasted seven days" (1 Samuel 31:11-13).

"And when all Jabesh Gilead heard all that the Philistines had done to Saul, all the valiant men arose and took the body of Saul and the bodies of his sons; and they brought them to Jabesh, and buried their bones under the tamarisk tree at Jabesh, and fasted seven days" (1 Chronicles 10:11-12).

"And they mourned and wept and fasted until evening for Saul and for Jonathan his son, for the people of the LORD and for the house of Israel, because they had fallen by the sword" (2 Samuel 1:12).

FASTING ON NATIONAL CALAMITIES

There are four significant events in the history of the Jews which necessitated regular or annual fasts. Without delving too much into the details of each fast, it must be noted that during and after the Exile, these fasts were observed as

Chapter 2 – Fasting in the Old Testament

memorials of the calamities that had befallen them at the time.

- The burning of the Temple: the fast of the tenth of the fifth month (Jeremiah 52:12-13).
- The murder of Gedaliah: the fast of the second day of the seventh month (2 Kings 25:23-95; Jeremiah 41:1ff).
- The beginning of the siege of Jerusalem: the fast of the tenth day of the tenth month (2 Kings 25:1).
- The fall of Jerusalem: the fast of the ninth day of the fourth month (2 Kings 25:3-4).

THE FAST TRACK

CHAPTER 3

TYPES OF FASTS

According to Isaiah 58, the only fast specifically requested by God is the one that He is pleased with. However, we can classify fasting based on a certain clear criterion.

THE NORMAL FAST

There is nothing inherently abnormal about fasting. Therefore a normal fast does not automatically become more meaningful than any other type.

A normal fast is a fast that involves complete abstention from all food but not water. This is when the person fasting will drink only water but no food or even food supplements irrespective of the duration of the fast. In a normal fast, no flavoured water can be consumed; only pure water.

The normal fast is the most common fast in scriptures.

THE PARTIAL FAST

Partial fast involves a restriction of some diet but not total abstention.

> *"In those days I, Daniel, was mourning three full weeks. I ate no pleasant food, no meat or wine came into my mouth, nor did I anoint myself at all, till three whole weeks were fulfilled"* (Daniel 10:2-3).

While we are on the subject of the fast that Daniel observed, let me quickly seize the opportunity to address some misunderstandings regarding his fast.

In some circles, the partial fast is also referred to as 'white' fast simply because Daniel said he did not eat meat or drink wine. It is assumed that Daniel had fruits or vegetables and probably without oil or salt. Those who follow this line said, 'no pleasant food' means, no tasty or fatty foods. The Daniel 10 reference was linked to an earlier passage from the same book where Daniel and his colleagues refused to partake of the king's delicacies which were

Chapter 3 – Types of Fasts

pleasant, meaty and certainly accompanied by a selection of Royal wine. Let's read it.

> *"But Daniel purposed in his heart that he would not defile himself with the portion of the king's delicacies, nor with the wine which he drank; therefore he requested of the chief of the eunuchs that he might not defile himself. So Daniel said to the steward whom the chief of the eunuchs had set over Daniel, Hananiah, Mishael, and Azariah, "Please test your servants for ten days, and let them give us vegetables to eat and water to drink. And at the end of ten days their features appeared better and fatter in flesh than all the young men who ate the portion of the king's delicacies"* (Daniel 1:8, 11-12, 15).

The problem with this Bible reference being used to justify 'white fast' are numerous. However, let's just observe a few.

According to Scripture, they did not choose to fast. They just refused to eat of the king's delicacies. The King wanted to feed them very extravagantly and have them trained for three years so they could be fit for royal duties.

Also, observe that they only did abstain from the king's delicacies for ten days to prove to the King that they could do without such food and still be healthy and strong. All the chosen men were henceforth commanded to be fed with Daniel's menu for the next three years. If they were fasting, then it lasted three years.

Thirdly, it is nowhere recorded that they were 'afflicting their souls' or that they were seeking the face of the Lord during this period of abstinence.

Finally, the latter reference in Daniel 10 conclusively stated that Daniel only abstained from delicacies to seek God's face for twenty-one days before and after which he must have fed differently.

The summary is that what people here regarded as partial or white fast was no fast. It was a period of self-denial to prove a point.

Those who prescribe the 'Daniel Fast' or 'White Fast' also usually recommend that it must be a twenty-one day fast just because Daniel fasted for 21 days. This is not my understanding of this passage in Daniel Chapter 10.

Yes, Daniel fasted for 21 days, but it was not his intention to fast for so long. He just wanted to fast to seek God's mind regarding Israel's

Chapter 3 – Types of Fasts

future. God heard his prayers and sent the answer from the very first day Daniel started fasting. It was a hindrance in the spiritual realm that delayed the manifestation of the answer. As Daniel continued to fast and to declare the word of God concerning His promises to Israel, Gabriel, the Archangel of Goodness, received strength through the support of Michael, the Archangel of War. Because of the synergy, Daniel received the reply to his request on the 21st day of fasting.

If we are to fast in the similitude of the 'Daniel Fast,' we must be prepared to fast for a shorter, exact or longer days than Daniel fasted. After all, like Daniel, we must continue to fast and should only stop fasting after we have received the answer to our request whether before, or after 21 days. This is the true meaning of the 'Daniel Fast.' It is a fast for as long as necessary.

THE ABSOLUTE FAST

As the name suggests, the absolute fast is a fast that excludes both food and drink. No water or food is allowed, and some activities may also have to be avoided. Most absolute fasts in the Bible are 'Called Fasts,' and are of national significance. In extreme cases as that of Nineveh, even the animals were denied food and drink. Let us take a look at a few scriptures relating to absolute fast. Their mention should provide sufficient understanding of the fast regarded as 'Absolute Fast.'

> *""Go, gather all the Jews who are present in Shushan, and fast for me; neither eat nor drink for three days, night or day. My maids and I will fast likewise. And so I will go to the king, which is against the law; and if I perish, I perish!"" (Esther 4:16).*

> *"When I went up into the mountain to receive the tablets of stone, the tablets of the covenant which the LORD made with you, then I stayed on the mountain forty days and forty nights. I neither ate bread nor drank water" (Deuteronomy 9:9).*

> *"So he arose, and ate and drank; and he went in the strength of that food forty days and forty nights as far as Horeb, the mountain of God" (1 Kings 19:8).*

Chapter 3 – Types of Fasts

"So the people of Nineveh believed God, proclaimed a fast, and put on sackcloth, from the greatest to the least of them. Then word came to the king of Nineveh; and he arose from his throne and laid aside his robe, covered himself with sackcloth and sat in ashes. And he caused it to be proclaimed and published throughout Nineveh by the decree of the king and his nobles, saying, Let neither man nor beast, herd nor flock, taste anything; do not let them eat, or drink water. But let man and beast be covered with sackcloth, and cry mightily to God; yes, let every one turn from his evil way and from the violence that is in his hands. Who can tell if God will turn and relent, and turn away from His fierce anger, so that we may not perish? Then God saw their works, that they turned from their evil way; and God relented from the disaster that He had said He would bring upon them, and He did not do it" (Jonah 3:5-10).

"And he was three days without sight, and neither ate nor drank" (Acts 9:9).

THE FAST TRACK

As earlier said, the absolute fast may require staying away from food, drinks and sexual intimacy.

> *"Do not deprive one another except with consent for a time, that you may give yourselves to fasting and prayer; and come together again so that Satan does not tempt you because of your lack of self-control"* (1 Corinthians 7:5)

CHAPTER 4

DURATION OF FASTS

There are no strict regulations regarding the length or duration of fasts to make it more meaningful and acceptable. An acceptable fast is not determined by its duration but by its quality and the motive behind it. A long fast is not more acceptable if the heart of the individual is impure than a short fast that reveres God. As in prayer, the length of a fast can be determined by some criteria.

God inspired - if God calls a fast, He will determine its length.

Circumstances - an example is to hear of a friend or loved one who is terminally ill and to determine to fast for God's mercy. You may fast until there is no more need to fast or until you have received an assurance of heaven's attention or until God stops you. King David prayed for son's health to be restored as long as the child was alive. He stopped fasting when the child died.

Purpose - there are different reasons to fast. Some of these are mentioned in a separate chapter. Seeking the face of God for directions may require a different duration compared to humbling yourself or afflicting your soul in repentance. Other reasons like fasting as a spiritual discipline, or restrictions based on health issues may determine the length of the fast.

Now let's look into various duration of fasts.

ONE NIGHT

The idea of missing dinner

> *"Now the king went to his palace and spent the night fasting; and no musicians were brought before him. Also his sleep went from him"* (Daniel 6:18).

UNTIL EVENING

David and his men fasted only until evening. This is the idea of missing lunch.

Chapter 4 – Duration of Fasts

"And they mourned and wept and fasted until evening for Saul and for Jonathan his son, for the people of the LORD and for the house of Israel, because they had fallen by the sword" (2 Samuel 1:12).

ONE DAY

From sunrise to sunset - food is taken after sundown. This is the idea of missing breakfast and lunch.

"And when all the people came to persuade David to eat food while it was still day, David took an oath, saying, "God do so to me, and more also, if I taste bread or anything else till the sun goes down!"" (2 Samuel 3:35).

"Then all the children of Israel, that is, all the people, went up and came to the house of God and wept. They sat there before the LORD and fasted that day until evening; and they offered burnt offerings and peace offerings before the LORD" (Judges 20:26).

THE FAST TRACK

TWICE IN A WEEK

The fast 'twice-a-week' is not commanded but was a genuinely difficult one. Done for the right reasons, it definitely can be one of the most powerful weapons against the flesh.

> *"I fast twice a week; I give tithes of all that I possess'" (Luke 18:12).*

THREE DAYS

> *""Go, gather all the Jews who are present in Shushan, and fast for me; neither eat nor drink for three days, night or day. My maids and I will fast likewise. And so I will go to the king, which is against the law; and if I perish, I perish!"" (Esther 4:16).*

> *"And he was three days without sight, and neither ate nor drank" (Acts 9:9).*

SEVEN DAYS

> *"Then they took their bones and buried them under the tamarisk tree at Jabesh, and fasted seven days" (2 Samuel 31:13).*

Chapter 4 – Duration of Fasts

"And when all Jabesh Gilead heard all that the Philistines had done to Saul, all the valiant men arose and took the body of Saul and the bodies of his sons; and they brought them to Jabesh, and buried their bones under the tamarisk tree at Jabesh, and fasted seven days" (1 Chronicles 10:11-12).

"So the elders of his house arose and went to him, to raise him up from the ground. But he would not, nor did he eat food with them. Then on the seventh day it came to pass that the child died. And the servants of David were afraid to tell him that the child was dead. For they said, "Indeed, while the child was alive, we spoke to him, and he would not heed our voice. How can we tell him that the child is dead? He may do some harm!"" (2 Samuel 12:17-18).

FOURTEEN DAYS

"Now when much time had been spent, and sailing was now dangerous because the Fast was already over, Paul advised them, saying, "Men, I perceive that this voyage will end with disaster and much

loss, not only of the cargo and ship, but also our lives." And as day was about to dawn, Paul implored them all to take food, saying, "Today is the fourteenth day you have waited and continued without food, and eaten nothing" (Acts 27:9-10, 33).

DANIEL FAST

No set time limit. See chapter on Daniel Fast.

"In those days I, Daniel, was mourning three full weeks. I ate no pleasant food, no meat or wine came into my mouth, nor did I anoint myself at all, till three whole weeks were fulfilled" (Daniel 10:2-3).

FORTY DAYS

The longest fasts recorded in Scripture were the forty day fasts by Moses, Elijah, and Jesus - Exodus 34:28; Deuteronomy 9:9; 1 Kings 19:8;

"And when He had fasted forty days and forty nights, afterward He was hungry" (Matthew 4:2).

"Being tempted for forty days by the devil. And in those days He ate nothing,

Chapter 4 – Duration of Fasts

and afterward, when they had ended, He was hungry" (Luke 4:2).

FASTED LIFE

It can be done nightly, daily, weekly, or whichever other regular practice, living a fasted life in the power of the Holy Spirit can be a powerful tool to fight and conquer the flesh. An example is Anna, the prophetess who fasted day and night for a long time. She possibly survived on one meal a day for 37 years.

> *"There was also a prophet, Anna, the daughter of Penuel, of the tribe of Asher. She was very old; she had lived with her husband seven years after her marriage, and then was a widow until she was eighty-four. She never left the temple but worshiped night and day, fasting and praying" (Luke 2:36-37 NIV).*

FASTING FOR BEGINNERS

> *"My knees are weak through fasting, and my flesh is feeble from lack of fatness" (Psalms 109:24).*

THE FAST TRACK

A normal Jewish fast is from dusk to dusk, but you should endeavour to fast from 12 midnight until 6pm daily.

If you have never fasted before, it is better to:

- Gradually win yourself off of stimulants like tea, coffee, caffeinated drinks and any food that can cause withdrawal symptoms.
- Start slowly and build up gradually. Start with just missing a meal; breakfast, lunch, or dinner, it does not matter. I have seen people dive into the deep end starting with absolute fast. That is wrong.
- Break carefully. During fasting, it is okay to feel tired. This is because your lost nutrients and energy have not been replenished and your sugar level would have dropped. When breaking your fast, it is essential not to rush into gobbling heavy meals. You want to avoid raising your sugar level.
- Break gradually. Start with fresh fruits and vegetables in small amounts.
- Take time to pray and meditate on the word of God.

Chapter 4 – Duration of Fasts

- Keep confessing God's word. This is what the angels act on (Psalms 103:20). Daniel said "… while I was speaking in prayer …" (Daniel 9:21), and the angel said "…, your words were heard; and I have come because of your words" (Daniel 10:12).
- Fast when you have time to spend in prayerful meditation and pray before breaking each day. Remember the purpose of fasting;
    - To humble oneself in God's sight
    - To seek favorable answer to prayer for some important plea
- If you are pregnant or on any form of medication, seek medical advice, but pray always

THE FAST TRACK

CHAPTER 5

JESUS' TEACHING ON FASTING

"WHEN YOU FAST..."

Jesus nowhere commanded people to fast but expected men everywhere to fast.

There were three exercises that were very traditional to the Jews that Jesus corrected: the exercise of prayer, giving and fasting. Those were common Jewish practices, but they were not rightly done. So He addressed those in His first recorded message - ' The Sermon on the Mount'. He did not cancel them but corrected them.

Giving - "Therefore, when you do a charitable deed" (Matthew 6:2). "But when you do a charitable deed" (Matthew 6:3).

Praying - "And when you pray" (Matthew 6:5, 7). "But you, when you pray" (Matthew 6:6).

THE FAST TRACK

Fasting - "Moreover, when you fast" (Matthew 6:18). "But you, when you fast" (Matthew 6:19).

In the last of those three instances, Jesus expected people to fast. He did not have to command it because it was a standard practice anyway. He only corrected the practice and the motive behind it.

EARTHLY REWARD VERSUS HEAVENLY REWARD

> *""Moreover, when you fast, do not be like the hypocrites, with a sad countenance. For they disfigure their faces that they may appear to men to be fasting. Assuredly, I say to you, they have their reward. But you, when you fast, anoint your head and wash your face, so that you do not appear to men to be fasting, but to your Father who is in the secret place; and your Father who sees in secret will reward you openly" (Matthew 6:16-18).*

Fasting can be done with hypocrisy or humility. Whichever way you choose to do your fasting, there is always a reward. The results of fasting according to Jesus can be very striking.

Chapter 5 – Jesus' Teaching on Fasting

- Both hypocritical and discreet fasts are rewarded openly; one is by men, and the other is by our Heavenly Father.
- One is physical only, but the other is spiritual but manifested in the physical.
- One is a wage, and the other is a gift.

The last point may be new to some of my readers. So let me explain.

Jesus said in verse 16, "they have their reward." The word translated 'reward' here is the Greek word *'misthos'* which means 'wages.' When you fast to appear before men to be fasting, all you get is a pay packet of praise and applause. This is the earthly reward, a wage.

The heavenly reward is different. Two verses later, Jesus mentioned that the "Father who sees in secret would reward you openly." The Greek word translated 'reward' is *'apodidomi'* meaning 'gift.' God the Father gives you a gift. It is unspecified, but I can assure you, it is a worthy gift.

This means the fast that guarantees earthly reward is based on works and effort. To earn more, you do more; the bigger reward is usually a result of bigger works. However, the fast that guarantees heavenly reward is based on grace and faith.

LOOK NORMAL

Jesus also taught that when we fast, we should look normal or even better than when we are not fasting.

> *""Moreover, when you fast, do not be like the hypocrites, with a sad countenance. For they disfigure their faces that they may appear to men to be fasting. Assuredly, I say to you, they have their reward. But you, when you fast, anoint your head and wash your face, so that you do not appear to men to be fasting, but to your Father who is in the secret place; and your Father who sees in secret will reward you openly" (Matthew 6:16-18).*

Fasting should be both private and personal, not a public display of piety. The exercise should not be easily detected. You should appear on the day of fast just as you would on other days. Perhaps if you decide to stay indoors or go to a retreat centre, you may choose to appear as you wish. However, if you have to appear in public, look as you always have, no sackcloth, no ashes.

Chapter 5 – Jesus' Teaching on Fasting

Here, Jesus was not saying you should not let people know about your fasting; He is saying you should not go about showing off.

Some people have the habit of breaking their fast when offered something to eat because they do not want to say they are fasting and so be like the hypocrite. Some would even give an excuse for not eating and lie in the process.

If you appear in public and are offered food while you are fasting, do not accept it and break your fast or lie to people about why you are not eating. Simply tell them you do not want to eat and if they ask why? Say you are fasting. You have not done anything wrong. Don't tell a lie.

THE UNNECESSARY FAST

Why fast when you are supposed to be feasting? Unless there is an urge or urgency to seek the face of the Lord in fasting and praying, you should not fast when you should be feasting. It is unnecessary. It may be unrewarding and can even be counterproductive. Jesus broke the tradition of men by not fasting unnecessarily. Notice I did not say irregularly; a discussion we shall have next. However, take a look at this scripture,

THE FAST TRACK

"Then the disciples of John came to Him, saying, "Why do we and the Pharisees fast often, but Your disciples do not fast?" And Jesus said to them, "Can the friends of the bridegroom mourn as long as the bridegroom is with them? But the days will come when the bridegroom will be taken away from them, and then they will fast. No one puts a piece of unshrunk cloth on an old garment; for the patch pulls away from the garment, and the tear is made worse. Nor do they put new wine into old wineskins, or else the wineskins break, the wine is spilled, and the wineskins are ruined. But they put new wine into new wineskins, and both are preserved"" (Matthew 9:14-17). Please see also Mark 2:18-20 and Luke 5:33-39.

John's disciples came to Jesus asking and wondering why His disciples are not as religious as they and the Pharisees. He told them simply; there was no need to fast just yet. He did not say to them not to fast; His reply was to show that a fast is pointless when it is unnecessary and that there will come a time when men will have no choice but to fast.

Chapter 5 – Jesus' Teaching on Fasting

REGULAR OR NOT

In the last scripture that we read, please notice, the disciples of John and the Pharisees had never given thought to the necessity of fasting. No. The question they asked was about its regularity and frequency. Traditionally, the Jews fasted twice a week; on Thursdays and Mondays. Those were the market days, and according to tradition also, Moses was believed to have ascended Mount Sinai on Thursday and descended on Monday. So they fasted regularly.

> *"Then the disciples of John came to Him, saying, "Why do we and the Pharisees fast often, but Your disciples do not fast?"" (Matthew 9:14).*

Although Jesus only here addressed the issue of purposeful fasting, He did not in any way condemned the frequency or regularity of it.

I have found in my experience that the most fruitful and productive fasts were the purposeful ones. They may be once weekly or seventy-two hours nonstop. Sometimes, it may be necessary to set a regular weekly or monthly period. If left open, most people would never fast. However, the most important thing is to fast on purpose.

THE FAST TRACK

THESE ARE THOSE DAYS

Corporate fasts in the Old Testament period were in response to tragedies or an impending calamities. They were also consecrated as calls to national repentance. For the Jews of Jesus' time, fasting carried on as a tradition, but His disciples did not fast because there were no national emergencies. While Jesus was present among them; there could not have been a tragedy He could not handle. It is therefore not surprising that when they were confronted with a ministry assignment, they could not do much because they were not fasting.

However, from the time of Jesus' ascension, it became imperative for His disciples and followers to fast. The presence of Jesus was to bring joy and rejoicing, and His absence was to spell doom. Access to Him was to be by faith and belief. From over two thousand years ago and until now, Christians are expected to contact heaven on their knees with fasting and praying. It is not a command but a necessity. These are the days Jesus spoke about in the Gospels.

> *"The disciples of John and of the Pharisees were fasting. Then they came and said to Him, "Why do the disciples of John and of*

Chapter 5 – Jesus' Teaching on Fasting

the Pharisees fast, but Your disciples do not fast?" And Jesus said to them, "Can the friends of the bridegroom fast while the bridegroom is with them? As long as they have the bridegroom with them they cannot fast. But the days will come when the bridegroom will be taken away from them, and then they will fast in those days. No one sews a piece of unshrunk cloth on an old garment; or else the new piece pulls away from the old, and the tear is made worse. And no one puts new wine into old wineskins; or else the new wine bursts the wineskins, the wine is spilled, and the wineskins are ruined. But new wine must be put into new wineskins"" (Mark 2:18-22). See also Matthew 9:14-17 and Luke 5:33-39.

THE FAST TRACK

CHAPTER 6

FASTING IN THE NEW TESTAMENT

Before we take an in-depth look at individual texts in the New Testament regarding fasting, let me summarise what the Bible teaches about New Testament fasting.

The fact that there are no references to fasting in the New Testament outside the Synoptic Gospels, Acts of Apostles and Corinthians would suggest that the Church did not consider the practice of fasting as important while the Apostles were alive.

The New Testament Epistles, save Paul's Epistles to the Corinthians, say nothing about religious fasting. Paul did not even mention fasting as an obligatory religious exercise.

Even surprising is the fact that the General Epistles (Hebrews; James; 1 and 2 Peter; 1, 2, and 3 John; Jude) and Revelation make no mention of fasting. More interesting is the lack of reference to fasting in Hebrews, James, and 1 Peter, which were addressed to Jewish Christians.

So, every knowledge to be gained from the New Testament regarding fasting will be drawn from passages appearing in the Gospels, the Book of Acts, and Paul's letters to the Corinthians, to which we now turn.

PROPHET ANNA FASTED 37 YEARS

She was Eighty-four when Jesus was born. Anna chose a celibate lifestyle after losing her husband whom she was married to for a very short period of seven years. For almost four decades, Anna dedicated her life to ministering unto God in the temple service. This is worth commending for a thirty-seven-year-old with her future ahead of her, to turn her back on the world and to focus on ministry work. She did this night and day worshipping, fasting and praying.

> *"There was also a prophet, Anna, the daughter of Penuel, of the tribe of Asher. She was very old; she had lived with her husband seven years after her marriage, and then was a widow until she was*

Chapter 6 – Fasting in the New Testament

eighty-four. She never left the temple but worshiped night and day, fasting and praying" (Luke 2:36-37 NIV).

JESUS FASTED 40 DAYS

"Then Jesus was led up by the Spirit into the wilderness to be tempted by the devil. And when He had fasted forty days and forty nights, afterward He was hungry" (Matthew 4:1-2).

"Then Jesus, being filled with the Holy Spirit, returned from the Jordan and was led by the Spirit into the wilderness, being tempted for forty days by the devil. And in those days He ate nothing, and afterward, when they had ended, He was hungry" (Luke 4:1-2).

JOHN'S DISCIPLES FASTED OFTEN

"Then the disciples of John came to Him, saying, "Why do we and the Pharisees fast often, but Your disciples do not fast?"" (Matthew 9:14).

THE FAST TRACK

JESUS' DISCIPLES DID NOT FAST

"The disciples of John and of the Pharisees were fasting. Then they came and said to Him, "Why do the disciples of John and of the Pharisees fast, but Your disciples do not fast?"" (Mark 2:18).

THE PHARISEES FASTED OFTEN

"Then they said to Him, "Why do the disciples of John fast often and make prayers, and likewise those of the Pharisees, but Yours eat and drink?"" (Luke 5:33).

A PHARISEE FASTED TWICE A WEEK

"""Two men went up to the temple to pray, one a Pharisee and the other a tax collector. The Pharisee stood and prayed thus with himself, 'God, I thank You that I am not like other men — extortioners, unjust, adulterers, or even as this tax collector. I fast twice a week; I give tithes of all that I possess'" (Luke 18:10-12).

Chapter 6 – Fasting in the New Testament

PAUL FASTED AN UNSPECIFIED LENGTH OF TIME

Although the scripture next is from Paul's Epistle to the Corinthians, the part that addressed his fasting as in choice abstinence from food and drink alludes to the references in the Book of Acts.

> *"In stripes, in imprisonments, in tumults, in labors, in sleeplessness, in fastings"* (2 Corinthians 6:5).

> *"In weariness and toil, in sleeplessness often, in hunger and thirst, in fastings often, in cold and nakedness"* (2 Corinthians 11:27).

In both of these passages, Paul mentioned fasting as a mark of his ministry and of his good standing as a minister of Christ.

There were times the Apostle did not eat because there was nothing to eat (1 Corinthians 4:11; Philippians 4:12) and there were times he refused to eat because he was fasting (Acts 9:9; 13:2-3; 14:23). These two parallel situations are recorded in the same verse of scripture.

THE FAST TRACK

PAUL FASTED 14 DAYS

According to the Book of Acts chapter 27, Apostle Paul and his company (including Dr. Luke) fasted for 14 days on their way to Italy.

> *"Now when much time had been spent, and sailing was now dangerous because the Fast was already over, Paul advised them, saying, "Men, I perceive that this voyage will end with disaster and much loss, not only of the cargo and ship, but also our lives." And as day was about to dawn, Paul implored them all to take food, saying, "Today is the fourteenth day you have waited and continued without food, and eaten nothing" (Acts 27:9-10, 33).*

PAUL FASTED THREE DAYS

Following his Damascus Road encounter, we read in Acts 9:8-9 that Paul "neither ate or drank."

> *"Then Saul arose from the ground, and when his eyes were opened he saw no one. But they led him by the hand and brought him into Damascus. And he was three*

Chapter 6 – Fasting in the New Testament

days without sight, and neither ate nor drank."

Initially, you would think the statement meant he could not or would not eat or drink because the Holy Spirit was working on him. However, that was not the case. Dr. Luke, the writer of Acts, said concerning Jesus in the Gospel bearing his name, that "He ate nothing" (Luke 4:2), implying that He fasted, "He was hungry." These are the same words used in the Book of Acts.

CORNELIUS FASTED FOUR DAYS

Though Cornelius was not a Christian at the time, he was obviously a devout man who worshiped the God of Israel. Because of the genuineness of his heart and his request, God listened to him and sent him help.

> *"So Cornelius said, "Four days ago I was fasting until this hour; and at the ninth hour I prayed in my house, and behold, a man stood before me in bright clothing, and said, 'Cornelius, your prayer has been heard, and your alms are remembered in the sight of God"* (Acts 10:30-31).

COMMISSIONING MINISTERS

There are two New Testament references to fasting and praying before commissioning ministers for a role. The Book of Acts recorded believers fasting before important decisions were made. In the two instances, the Apostles felt the need to release people into ministry after observing a proper spiritual separation. These happened to the brethren in Antioch and the Churches in Galatia.

- Sending out missionaries - The Antioch Churches

Corporate prayers and fasting were done by the Apostles.

> *"Now in the church that was at Antioch, there were certain prophets and teachers: Barnabas, Simeon who was called Niger, Lucius of Cyrene, Manaen who had been brought up with Herod the tetrarch, and Saul. As they ministered to the Lord and fasted, the Holy Spirit said, "Now separate to Me Barnabas and Saul for the work to which I have called them." Then, having fasted and prayed, and laid hands on them, they sent them away" (Acts 13:1-3).*

Chapter 6 – Fasting in the New Testament

- Appointing Elders - The Galatians churches

Corporate prayers and fasting were done not just by a group of Apostles, but also by a group of churches.

> *"And when they had preached the gospel to that city and made many disciples, they returned to Lystra, Iconium, and Antioch, strengthening the souls of the disciples, exhorting them to continue in the faith, and saying, "We must through many tribulations enter the kingdom of God." So when they had appointed elders in every church, and prayed with fasting, they commended them to the Lord in whom they had believed" (Acts 14:21-23).*

FASTING AND SEXUAL INTIMACY

Paul stated in unequivocal terms the incompatibility of sex, prayer, and fasting. It is fair to say that, as a married man myself, it is so difficult to give undivided attention to your spouse and give yourself wholeheartedly to God, at the same time. You do either but not the two at the same time. This is consistent with the Old Testament practice of staying away from sexual contact days before approaching God. Though sex in the context of legal marriage is holy, it is difficult to offer your full devotion to God and at the same time be sexually available to your spouse.

> *"Do not deprive one another except with consent for a time, that you may give yourselves to fasting and prayer; and come together again so that Satan does not tempt you because of your lack of self-control"* (1 Corinthians 7:5).

> *"So Moses went down from the mountain to the people and sanctified the people, and they washed their clothes. And he said to the people, "Be ready for the third day; do not come near your wives." Then it came to pass on the third day, in the morning, that there were thunderings and lightning, and a thick cloud on the mountain; and the sound of the trumpet was thunderous so that all the people who were in the camp trembled. And Moses brought the people out of the camp to meet with God, and they stood at the foot of the mountain"* (Exodus 19:14-17).

Chapter 6 – Fasting in the New Testament

If you decide to fast, it is advisable not to go on such fast for longer than you or your spouse would be able to hold on without intimacy. Paul said that the devil could take advantage of your burning passion and you may be led the wrong path, if you stay away too long from sexual intimacy with your spouse because of fasting.

THE FAST TRACK

CHAPTER 7

FASTING FOR POWER

There seem to be a huge misunderstanding in the Pentecostal circle that anyone desiring to enter into full-time power ministry should (and in some cases, must) observe absolute fast continuously for forty days. There cannot be anything else further from the truth. While there is enough evidence to show and demonstrate that power manifestation and demonstration can be traced to some form of fasting, there is also a body of proof to the contrary. Arguably, Jesus insinuated that some level of operation requires the exercise of fasting (Matthew 17:17-21; Mark 9:23-29), yet there was no direct inference as to the nature, frequency or length of such discipline, and certainly not as a condition to obtaining power. After His discourse, it is nowhere noted that His disciples engaged in such long fast, yet they performed miracles still today unparalleled.

First, let us deal with the Matthew and Mark scriptures about fasting and prayer as a prerequisite to power ministry.

An Epileptic was brought to Jesus to be healed but because Jesus was attending to other people, the ministry responsibility landed on the lap of the disciples. After much effort, the boy could not be delivered. So the family had to wait until Jesus was available to heal him. From Matthews's Gospel, we learn the following:

> *"Then Jesus answered and said, "O faithless and perverse generation, how long shall I be with you? How long shall I bear with you? Bring him here to Me." And Jesus rebuked the demon, and it came out of him; and the child was cured from that very hour. Then the disciples came to Jesus privately and said, "Why could we not cast it out?" So Jesus said to them, "Because of your unbelief, for assuredly, I say to you, if you have faith as a mustard seed, you will say to this mountain, 'Move from here to there,' and it will move; and nothing will be*

Chapter 7 – Fasting for Power

impossible for you. However, this kind does not go out except by prayer and fasting" (Matthew 17-17-21).

Jesus did not rebuke his disciples for not being able to cure the boy. He instead rebuked the multitude as "faithless and perverse."

The disciples were not ashamed to have failed, so they boldly but quietly went to ask Jesus why they could not heal the boy.

Firstly, we must realise the place of faith as a key. The boy could have been healed by the disciples if they had exercised sufficient faith. It was "because of your unbelief," Jesus said. He also said, 'if you have faith as a mustard seed… nothing will be impossible for you.' The word 'nothing' here includes healing the epileptic, meaning that they could have healed the boy by faith.

Secondly, we need to also observe from Jesus's responses that not all power ministry require the practice of fasting. Saying 'this kind' signifies that there are other issues that can be dealt with without fasting.

From Mark's Gospel, we read,

"Jesus said to him, "If you can believe, all things are possible to him who believes."

> *Immediately the father of the child cried out and said with tears, "Lord, I believe; help my unbelief!" When Jesus saw that the people came running together, He rebuked the unclean spirit, saying to it: "Deaf and dumb spirit, I command you, come out of him and enter him no more!" Then the spirit cried out, convulsed him greatly, and came out of him. And he became as one dead, so that many said, "He is dead." But Jesus took him by the hand and lifted him up, and he arose. And when He had come into the house, His disciples asked Him privately, "Why could we not cast it out?" So He said to them, "This kind can come out by nothing but prayer and fasting" (Mark 9:23-29).*

The only difference in this story and Matthew's account is the fact that the father of the child was blamed for unbelief. Nothing was blamed on the disciples and certainly not for their lack of fasting.

In another instance, Jesus did not expect His disciples to be fasting.

> *"Then the disciples of John came to Him, saying, "Why do we and the Pharisees*

fast often, but Your disciples do not fast?" And Jesus said to them, "Can the friends of the bridegroom mourn as long as the bridegroom is with them? But the days will come when the bridegroom will be taken away from them, and then they will fast. No one puts a piece of unshrunk cloth on an old garment; for the patch pulls away from the garment, and the tear is made worse. Nor do they put new wine into old wineskins, or else the wineskins break, the wine is spilled, and the wineskins are ruined. But they put new wine into new wineskins, and both are preserved"" (Matthew 9:14-17). *Please see also Mark 2:18-20 and Luke 5:33-39.*

To acquire a better understanding of the purpose of the forty-day fasts in scripture, let us now turn to Bible references used by its proponents.

MOSES DID NOT EAT OR DRINK (40 DAYS AND 40 DAYS)

"So he was there with the LORD forty days and forty nights; he neither ate bread nor drank water. And He wrote on the

tablets the words of the covenant, the Ten Commandments" (Exodus 34:28).

"When I went up into the mountain to receive the tablets of stone, the tablets of the covenant which the LORD made with you, then I stayed on the mountain forty days and forty nights. I neither ate bread nor drank water" (Deuteronomy 9:9).

"And I fell down before the LORD, as at the first, forty days and forty nights; I neither ate bread nor drank water, because of all your sin which you committed in doing wickedly in the sight of the LORD, to provoke Him to anger" (Deuteronomy 9:18).

ELIJAH DID NOT EAT FOR 40 DAYS

"So he arose, and ate and drank; and he went in the strength of that food forty days and forty nights as far as Horeb, the mountain of God" (1 Kings 19:8).

Chapter 7 – Fasting for Power

JESUS FASTED 40 DAYS

> *"Then Jesus was led up by the Spirit into the wilderness to be tempted by the devil. And when He had fasted forty days and forty nights, afterward He was hungry"* (Matthew 4:1-2).

> *"Then Jesus, being filled with the Holy Spirit, returned from the Jordan and was led by the Spirit into the wilderness, being tempted for forty days by the devil. And in those days He ate nothing, and afterward, when they had ended, He was hungry"* (Luke 4:1-2).

These I have to say of the three scriptures regarding the fasts by Moses, Elijah, and Jesus.

Moses here never intended to fast for power. He was not even aware he needed more power since he had already performed awesome miracles for over ten months before this time without a single day fast. Moses only went to meet with God to receive further instructions regarding their journey to Canaan. The Bible did not say either that he knew how long he was going to be in God's presence. So he could not have planned a 40-day fast. However, when he was there, God made sure he did not feel any hunger for the length of time his attention was required. Call it supernatural? Yes.

What about Elijah? Even Elijah did not fast; he just did not eat because there was nothing to eat. It was not a choice not to eat for the purpose of becoming more powerful. He was already powerful, performing awesome miracles before this period. In fact, he was running away for fear of being killed. When he became tired and weary following a day's journey, an angel fed him so he could have strength for his next journey that would last forty days.

Concerning Jesus, the Bible made it clear that the purpose of His wilderness experience was to be tempted by the devil, not to fast to receive power. Even though he fasted, it was to destroy the power of the enemy who deceived Adam and Eve in the Garden of Eden into eating forbidden fruit. Jesus also did not need to fast to become powerful. As God in the flesh, He was already powerful. When you have the Holy Spirit, you have power (Acts 1:8), which was why Jesus performed awesome miracles. He was anointed with the Holy Spirit and power (Acts 10:38). The Bible said the Holy Spirit was on

Chapter 7 – Fasting for Power

Him before He went into the wilderness and the Holy Spirit led Him into the wilderness.

Now then, what was the significance of the three with regards to 40 days without food? Please follow me, and I will show you.

It is interesting to note that among many notable Bible figures only these three appeared at the mount of transfiguration, Jesus being already present.

> *"Then it happened, as they were parting from Him, that Peter said to Jesus, 'Master, it is good for us to be here; and let us make three tabernacles: one for You, one for Moses, and one for Elijah' not knowing what he said"* (Luke 9:33).

Why did Moses and Elijah show up at Transfiguration with Jesus? Their appearance at the transfiguration was the culmination of the three-dimensional role of the believer; the Priest, the Prophet, and the King or as some put it; the Law, the Prophets and the Grace of God. These are represented by the ministries of Moses the priest, Elijah the prophet and Jesus the King. The three roles are also epitomised in Jesus.

Only these three individuals were noted in the Bible to have individually 'fasted' (not eating) for forty days.

TWO THINGS WE NEED TO HIGHLIGHT.

Firstly, of the three, only Jesus fasted before He started ministry, the others two fasted after they were already in ministry. This means there are no biblical grounds for someone to fast for forty days before they enter into ministry.

Secondly, of the three, Jesus fasted in the wilderness, but Moses and Elijah fasted on the mountain. Again there are no biblical grounds for going to a 'mountain top' to fast for forty days. Your prayers are accepted based on your heart disposition and not on your physical location.

YOU ARE ALREADY POWERFUL

Elisha performed more miracles than Elijah, yet it is nowhere recorded that he fasted for one day let alone forty days.

Please also note, there were lots of other miracles recorded in the Old Testament without any link to a special forty days fast.

Chapter 7 – Fasting for Power

Coming to the New Testament, none of the Apostles were recorded to have fasted longer than three days, yet the power of God moved mightily through them. These are some of the recorded miracles performed by the apostles.

- All manner of sicknesses and diseases - Mark 6:7, 12-13; 16:15-20; Luke 9:1-2, 6; Acts 5:12-16; 6:8; 8:5-8; 19:11-12; 28:8-9
- Crippled (Impotence in feet) - Acts 14:8-10
- Fever - Acts 28:8-9
- Haemorrhage - Acts 28:8-9
- Lameness - Acts 3:1-10;
- Palsy - Acts 9:32-34

Amongst the Apostles, Paul fasted the longest which was only fourteen days.

> *"Now when much time had been spent, and sailing was now dangerous because the Fast was already over, Paul advised them, saying, "Men, I perceive that this voyage will end with disaster and much loss, not only of the cargo and ship, but also our lives." And as day was about to dawn, Paul implored them all to take food, saying, "Today is the fourteenth day you*

have waited and continued without food, and eaten nothing" (Acts 27:9-10, 33).

If a Christian feels led to observe the forty-day fast, he has not done wrong. Any length of fast does not change God in any shape or form. The forty-day fast may be necessary for the individual who feels called in the order of Moses, Elijah and Jesus, otherwise, it may be an unfruitful soulish exercise. Though the individual may begin to express greater manifestation of power, it is likely that same can be achieved with a shorter length of fast.

The power of God latent in a Christian is only aligned toward manifestation by the exercise of fasting, not by the length of the fast. You are already powerful. Fasting sharpens the spirit as filing sharpens the saw.

Those who were consecrated as ministers of the gospel were sent forth by the laying on of hands, prayer and fasting, not as individuals but as a community of believers and certainly no longer than a few days fast.

"Now in the church that was at Antioch there were certain prophets and teachers: Barnabas, Simeon who was called Niger, Lucius of Cyrene, Manaen who had been

Chapter 7 – Fasting for Power

brought up with Herod the tetrarch, and Saul. As they ministered to the Lord and fasted, the Holy Spirit said, "Now separate to Me Barnabas and Saul for the work to which I have called them." Then, having fasted and prayed, and laid hands on them, they sent them away" (Acts 13:1-3).

"And when they had preached the gospel to that city and made many disciples, they returned to Lystra, Iconium, and Antioch, strengthening the souls of the disciples, exhorting them to continue in the faith, and saying, "We must through many tribulations enter the kingdom of God." So when they had appointed elders in every church, and prayed with fasting, they commended them to the Lord in whom they had believed" (Acts 14:21-23).

Finally, you do not have to fast to be acceptable to God. Enoch, Moses, Elijah, and Jesus are the only ones who cannot be found in their graves. They are recorded in the Bible to have been translated to heaven in one form or another. Except for Enoch, the rest three of them 'fasted' (did not eat) for forty days. Enoch only walked with God, and he was no more. He did not have to fast for forty days in other to please God or become more powerful.

God is more interested in who we are than in what we do. I have seen a countless number of people claiming they have fasted for forty days and you would be amazed why their life is not changed. Their claimed experience with God did not change their character.

If you have fasted for forty days and have received power, I am sure your flesh and its deed would have been mortified during the period, so your spirit was aligned with the Spirit of God.

CHAPTER 8

THE SHALLOW FAST

Have you ever fasted and prayed and wondered why your prayers go unanswered? It is possible that your fasting has gone unnoticed by God. Let us explore this possibility from the most popular scripture on fasting in the entire Bible, the whole of Isaiah 58.

> *"Cry aloud, spare not; lift up your voice like a trumpet; tell My people their transgression, and the house of Jacob their sins. They seek Me daily, and delight to know My ways, as a nation that did righteousness, and did not forsake the ordinance of their God. They ask of Me the ordinances of justice; they take delight in approaching God. "Why have we fasted," they say, "and You have not seen? Why have we afflicted our souls,*

and You take no notice?" (Isaiah 58:1-3a).

The Jews became frustrated about not being heard by God. They felt God had been unfair to them. So they poured their hearts to God and boasted about their self righteousness:

- We seek You daily;
- We delight to know Your ways;
- We are a nation that practice righteousness;
- We have not forsaken Your ordinances;
- We sought to know Your ordinances of justice; and
- We delight in approaching You;

In later verses, we see even more boasting.

"Is it a fast that I have chosen, a day for a man to afflict his soul? Is it to bow down his head like a bulrush, and to spread out sackcloth and ashes? Would you call this a fast, and an acceptable day to the LORD?" (Isaiah 58:5).

- We afflicted our souls;
- We bowed down our heads like a bulrush; and

Chapter 8 – The Shallow Fast

- We spread out sack cloths and slept inside ashes;

So what is all that about? We even fasted and You, our God, have not seen us? Doesn't our afflicted souls show before the throne?

Some people fast to show how holy and pious they can be, and to their shame feel unnoticed by God. They seem to forget that only men can be pleased with outward appearances. When we attend public functions and perform certain public rites, they can go only as far as impressing a mortal like us. Not so with God.

The Jews had the appearance of a holy and righteous nation which loved God and were devotedly seeking Him daily. They came across as a people that delighted in approaching God, and seeking His mind concerning justice, afflicted their souls in fasting. All that went unnoticed by God.

In answer, God was direct about the reason He hid His face from them. No beating around the bush. Reality is about to be more real. Forget about the image, let us talk about the damage. God cuts to the chase. Their actions were right, but their heart attitude was wrong. Outwardly, they went enviable, but inwardly they were pitiable.

THE FAST TRACK

Many people do the right things but do the right things wrongly. When you fast the right way, your sacrifice will become acceptable. Fasting with the wrong attitude is just a waste of time and unproductive. It is simply a hunger strike. Though you are visible, you become unnoticeable, and your good intentions are not going to be rewarded by God. All of it is a religious veneer, an empty ritual. This kind of fasting is braggadocios, empty, hollow, and lacks any spiritual substance behind it.

> *"In fact, in the day of your fast you find pleasure, and exploit all your labourers. Indeed you fast for strife and debate, and to strike with the fist of wickedness. You will not fast as you do this day, to make your voice heard on high. Is it a fast that I have chosen, a day for a man to afflict his soul? Is it to bow down his head like a bulrush, and to spread out sackcloth and ashes? Would you call this a fast, and an acceptable day to the LORD?" (Isaiah 58:3b-5).*

The employers were covetous and unmerciful. It is unthinkable that someone described as righteous would be unkind to, cheat, and exploit

Chapter 8 – The Shallow Fast

his or her staff and find pleasure in doing so. It is grossly unacceptable. That carried on even on a day they are fasting and seemed even to relish the experience. Where is the fear of God? How can you say you are an obedient child of God when your fasting is disconnected from fairness? It just doesn't add up. It is hypocrisy of the first order.

Writing in 1832, Adam Clarke said, and I quote,

> *"How can any nation pretend to fast or worship God at all, or dare to profess that they believe in the existence of such a Being, while they carry on the slave trade, and traffic in the souls, blood, and bodies of men! O ye most flagitious of knaves, and worst of hypocrites, cast off at once the mask of your religion; and deepen not your endless perdition by professing the faith of our Lord Jesus Christ, while ye continue in this traffic!"*

Apart from exploitation, some of their reasons for fasting were hideous. They were fasting to win arguments and to defeat an opponent, possibly another Jew, in the court of law, and about whose sin is worst. Certainly, I would be flabbergasted – fasting for contentions, spite, conflicts, disputes, and fighting of all sorts? Added to these, they fasted so they could inflict unjust injuries on those who are against their unjust acts.

When your fasting is soulish, and your prayers are selfish as to ask God to help you defeat an enemy while you are also described as wicked, God will not answer.

When your fasting is toward self-glorification; a request to make your voice louder than those of others, God may say "No." He does not regard that as fasting.

During the time of Jesus, a similar pride by a Pharisee was denounced in the parable of the Pharisee and the Publican.

> *"9 Also He spoke this parable to some who trusted in themselves that they were righteous and despised others: 10 "Two men went up to the temple to pray, one a Pharisee and the other a tax collector. 11 The Pharisee stood and prayed thus with himself, 'God, I thank You that I am not like other men - extortioners, unjust, adulterers, or even as this tax collector. 12 I fast twice a week; I give tithes of all*

Chapter 8 – The Shallow Fast

that I possess.' 13 And the tax collector, standing afar off, would not so much as raise his eyes to heaven, but beat his breast, saying, 'God, be merciful to me a sinner!'" (Luke 18:9-13).

There is a striking similarity in this story of the Pharisee with that of the people in Isaiah's day. He claimed,

- He was righteous;
- He fasted twice a week; and
- He gave tithes of all he possessed.

The Pharisee trusted in his empty rituals apart from the spiritual realism which is pictured in true repentance and devoid of self-aggrandisement and warped self-image.

If you fast and the focus is to exalt rather than humble yourself before God, the same judgement pronounced on the Pharisee by Jesus certainly may be said about you. It is pure hypocrisy. The Scripture declared,

"14 I tell you, this man went down to his house justified rather than the other; for everyone who exalts himself will be humbled, and he who humbles himself will be exalted" (Luke 18:14).

THE FAST TRACK

GOD CANNOT BE FOOLED

Some people think they can disobey God, live anyhow they wish and then fast to obtain His favour. God cannot be mocked. That fast is just not going to be accepted. Fasting cannot twist God's arms, particularly when He had requested obedience. He desires obedience than fasting. The truth of the matter is that most fasts will be unnecessary if men will obey God's instructions. Do you not think that if you are not ready to do His will, your fasting will not be accepted?

The children of Israel fasted year after year during the fifth and seventh months for seventy years, yet they refused to obey God's instructions. They turned fasting into an external show and a ceremonial ritual. Let's read Zechariah 7, verses 5-7 and 11-14 to get an idea of what can happen when we disobey God's laws and instructions and expect Him to be moved with our fasting. The prophet spoke against their spirituality.

> *""Say to all the people of the land, and to the priests: 'When you fasted and mourned in the fifth and seventh months during those seventy years, did you fast for Me - for Me? Really? When you eat*

Chapter 8 – The Shallow Fast

and when you drink, do you not eat and drink for yourselves? Should you not have obeyed the words which the LORD proclaimed through the former prophets when Jerusalem and the cities around it were inhabited and prosperous, and the South and the Lowland were inhabited?'"

"But they refused to heed, shrugged their shoulders, and stopped their ears so that they could not hear. Yes, they made their hearts like flint, refusing to hear the law and the words which the LORD of hosts had sent by His Spirit through the former prophets. Thus great wrath came from the LORD of hosts. Therefore it happened, that just as He proclaimed and they would not hear, so they called out and I would not listen," says the LORD of hosts. "But I scattered them with a whirlwind among all the nations which they had not known. Thus the land became desolate after them, so that no one passed through or returned; for they made the pleasant land desolate"" (Zechariah 7:5-7, 11-14).

THE FAST TRACK

Moving to Chapter eight of Zechariah, the Bible detailed in the entire chapter, the promises, and blessings God intended to pour out unto His children. To receive the promises, they had to love the truth and peace.

> *"These are the things you shall do: Speak each man the truth to his neighbor; Give judgment in your gates for truth, justice, and peace; Let none of you think evil in your heart against your neighbor; and do not love a false oath. For all these are things that I hate,' Says the LORD." Then the word of the LORD of hosts came to me, saying, "Thus says the LORD of hosts: 'The fast of the fourth month, The fast of the fifth, The fast of the seventh, And the fast of the tenth, Shall be joy and gladness and cheerful feasts For the house of Judah. Therefore love truth and peace'"* (Zechariah 8:16-19).

WASTED FAST

We see from Jeremiah chapters 13 and 14 that our fasting will not be accepted it we keep disobeying God's laws.

Chapter 8 – The Shallow Fast

"When they fast, I will not hear their cry; and when they offer burnt offering and grain offering, I will not accept them. But I will consume them by the sword, by the famine, and by the pestilence"" (Jeremiah 14:12).

Do not engage in the exercise of fasting if your ways are not pure before God. He promised He would not even listen to your cry.

So far in this chapter, I have highlighted the don'ts of fasting and let us face it, nobody like do-nots. It is negative. It puts people on the defensive and perhaps that is what you have done. You have been defending yourself over every point that I have made up to this point. That is not my mission, but I trust that if you have been touched in any way, it is so that your fasting henceforth can be productive, noticed and acceptable. That is why we fast, isn't it? We fast to be fruitful, noticed and accepted.

Let us now turn to the dos of fasting in the following chapter.

THE FAST TRACK

CHAPTER 9

ACCEPTABLE FAST

Coming away from all despicable devotion to shallow fasts, we now turn to see God's chosen way of fasting. It is not that God was or is against fasting. No. He was just not pleased with the hypocrisy that surrounded the sacrifice. After all, it is a sacrifice. God sees through the spiritual veneer and the empty religious ritual many people have made of fasting and He is trying to get us on the right path of true and godly, genuine and humble fast that is seen, successful, and satisfying.

Reading from Isaiah 58:6-7, we noticed the characteristics of the Acceptable Fast and how it may apply to us.

> *"Is this not the fast that I have chosen: to loose the bonds of wickedness, to undo the*

> *heavy burdens, to let the oppressed go free, and that you break every yoke? Is it not to share your bread with the hungry, and that you bring to your house the poor who are cast out; when you see the naked, that you cover him, and not hide yourself from your own flesh?" (Isaiah 58:6-7).*

TO LOOSE THE BONDS OF WICKEDNESS

God is telling us to stop oppressing our brothers and sisters; to stop oppressing each other and to start reaching out to help those who are oppressed. If we are serious about fasting in the way that pleases Him, we must begin to get right with our brothers and sisters. This means no more trying to get even with each other. It means we have to stop acting wickedly towards each other; getting right with God and stopping the evil we do towards our brethren. To loose the bonds of wickedness is to fight for the cause of those on the receiving end of wickedness.

TO UNDO THE HEAVY BURDENS

There are people who would not lift a finger yet expect their employee to do all their biddings. Not only that, they put so much demand on them like putting a burden on a

Chapter 9 – Acceptable Fast

mule or horse, more than it can carry, under which it is ready to sink. What a shame that God had to rebuke them? As children of God, they should have known better.

God wants us to be careful not to lay on the back of our subordinate things that are heavy for them to bear. Jesus said in Matthew 23:1-7,

> *"1 Then Jesus spoke to the multitudes and to His disciples, 2 saying: "The scribes and the Pharisees sit in Moses' seat. 3 Therefore whatever they tell you to observe, that observe and do, but do not do according to their works; for they say, and do not do. 4 For they bind heavy burdens, hard to bear, and lay them on men's shoulders; but they themselves will not move them with one of their fingers. 5 But all their works they do to be seen by men. They make their phylacteries broad and enlarge the borders of their garments. 6 They love the best places at feasts, the best seats in the synagogues, 7 greetings in the marketplaces, and to be called by men, 'Rabbi, Rabbi.'"*

Their actions were atrocious, to say the least.

The point is this; you should not ask other people to do things you would not do. To undo the heavy burden means to take the loads off the shoulders of the poor and vulnerable. This is what fasting is about.

TO LET THE OPPRESSED GO FREE

Letting the oppressed go free is at the heart of any fast. Oppression makes life bitter for the oppressed. To be in a state where you actually can be oppressed is already dehumanising. No human creature of God should be treated so coldheartedly. Following after Master Jesus' mission, we are supposed to let the oppressed go.

> *"18 The Spirit of the Lord is upon Me, because He has anointed Me to preach the gospel to the poor; He has sent Me to heal the broken-hearted, to proclaim liberty to the captives and recovery of sight to the blind, to set at liberty those who are oppressed; 19 To proclaim the acceptable year of the Lord" (Luke 4:18-19).*

> *"38 How God anointed Jesus of Nazareth with the Holy Spirit and with power, who*

Chapter 9 – Acceptable Fast

went about doing good and healing all who were oppressed by the devil, for God was with Him" (Acts 10:38).

Freeing the oppressed – that is what Jesus did, and this is what we must do.

TO BREAK EVERY YOKE

Fasting should prick the hearts of those fasting towards breaking the yokes of slavery and assisting those wrongfully yoked. It is useless to fast if one of the intentions is not to break yokes. Yokes are necessary to be broken, not only removed and those under the yokes being temporarily released. Breaking the yoke is to ensure that the yoked have no fear of being re-yoked in the future. Every yoke must be broken with none left.

Ironically, Jesus invited us to take on a different lighter yoke for our spiritual training and development.

> *"28 Come to Me, all you who labour and are heavy laden, and I will give you rest. 29 Take My yoke upon you and learn from Me, for I am gentle and lowly in heart, and you will find rest for your*

souls. 30 For My yoke is easy and My burden is light" (Matthew 11:28-30).

SHARE YOUR BREAD WITH THE HUNGRY

Fasting God's way demands that we be generous to those that stand in need of assistance. Those that qualify for the loosening of bonds of wickedness, the undoing of the heavy burdens, the letting go of the oppressed, and the breaking of the yoke, also qualify for charitable acts.

When such individuals fast, they must also act lovingly towards other people, especially the needy, and to feed those that want food.

Feeding should be from profit honestly gained. "Thy bread," it said. We are not to feed the poor from substances stolen from them in the first place. It should not be from the proceeds of oppression, burdening employees, heavy laden, or yokes. It should be from goods acquired from the work of one's hands. That is the basis of charitable deed according to Ephesians 4:28.

> *"28 Let him who stole steal no longer, but rather let him labour, working with his hands what is good, that he may have something to give him who has need."*

Chapter 9 – Acceptable Fast

This sometimes requires that we deny ourselves, so that we may have something to give to the needy. When we fast, the "bread" that we have saved during the fast or the value of it should at least be given to the poor. It is even better to fast deliberately so we can give to the needy. That will be a novelty and a brilliant idea.

We are also admonished to share our bread, not bread crumbs or scraps of food. Giving to the poor is purposely breaking bread for them as a show of care and love, not a demonstration of pity concerning their state. This is true fast.

BRING THE POOR TO YOUR HOUSE

Our fast will include an act of sheltering the homeless by providing lodging for those that want it. When the oppressed are set free, their burdens removed, their heavy laden lightened, and their yokes have been broken, it is suggestive that they may need not only bread to eat but also a house to live in, even if temporarily. It may simply mean paying for their housing or offering them space in your already crowded accommodation, which is a bigger sacrifice and a greater act of kindness. Unknowingly, many have entertained angels unaware or entertain Christ himself unintentionally building up a future recompense in the process.

> *"Do not forget to entertain strangers, for by so doing some have unwittingly entertained angels" (Hebrews 13:2).*

> *"37 "Then the righteous will answer Him, saying, 'Lord, when did we see You hungry and feed You, or thirsty and give You drink? 38 When did we see You a stranger and take You in, or naked and clothe You? 39 Or when did we see You sick, or in prison, and come to You?' 40 And the King will answer and say to them, 'Assuredly, I say to you, inasmuch as you did it to one of the least of these My brethren, you did it to Me'" (Matthew 25:37-40).*

COVER THOSE WITHOUT CLOTHING

Fasting goes further to include clothing the needy. After the fortune of the oppressed has been released, their burdens have been removed or lessened, their yokes have been shattered, their life is incomplete without food, shelter, and

Chapter 9 – Acceptable Fast

clothing on their back. With food, the needy will look physically nourished, with housing, he will be protected from the effects and harms of the harsh weather, and with cloth, he will appear decorously among his friends and attend fellowship.

If it is within your means to be charitable to those who want it, yet you refuse, there is no meaning to your fast. They will not be seen, successful and satisfying.

> *"Do not withhold good from those to whom it is due, when it is in the power of your hand to do so" (Proverbs 3:27).*

> *"Whoever shuts his ears to the cry of the poor will also cry himself and not be heard" (Proverbs 21:13).*

TO NOT HIDE FROM YOUR FLESH

If fasting away from family is what you like, take a look again at God's instruction. Many try to get away from distractions which are great when you know focusing can be an issue. However, this can never make you more spiritual. It only helps you to concentrate on fasting. I come from a background that places more value on 'mountain top' prayers and fasting as a means of attaining a greater level of spirituality. No, it will not make you more spiritual than if you were staying at home with your immediate family. You can be as distracted away from home as much as you can be at home.

You could not fulfil any of the characteristics of the acceptable fast without being among people. How would you be able to loose the bonds of wickedness, undo the heavy burdens, let the oppressed go free, break every yoke, share your bread with the hungry, bring to your house the poor who are cast out; and when you see the naked, cover him while fasting in seclusion.

You may say, 'but didn't Jesus say that you should be secretive or discreet when you engage in spiritual exercises of fasting?' He certainly did, but not the way it is popularly interpreted. He was only addressing those who are dramatic. Take a look at it here.

> *"16 "Moreover, when you fast, do not be like the hypocrites, with a sad countenance. For they disfigure their faces that they may appear to men to be fasting. Assuredly, I say to you, they have their*

Chapter 9 – Acceptable Fast

reward. 17 But you, when you fast, anoint your head and wash your face, 18 so that you do not appear to men to be fasting, but to your Father who is in the secret place; and your Father who sees in secret will reward you openly" (Matthew 6:16-18).

Did you see the words "they disfigure their faces that they may appear to men to be fasting?" Yes, that is right; their motive for fasting was to show off.

Then Jesus said,

17 "But you, when you fast, anoint your head and wash your face, 18 so that you do not appear to men to be fasting."

There is no point anointing your head and washing your face if you were only going to stay at home or away from people. I do not bother so much about that when I am staying at home.

Concerning the secret place, what was Jesus saying? Certainly, not a physical location somewhere as you would not interpret the 'secret place' in Psalm 91 as one isolated geographical location. It is the presence of God, which is nowhere but everywhere. God is everywhere.

It means that you do not go around telling everyone that you are fasting but keep such a secret by anointing your head and washing your face. No sackcloth and no sad countenance but a cheerful appearance. The Father Who lives in the 'secret place' and Who 'sees in secret' will reward you openly. The people in Isaiah's day wanted God to see them fasting, but He did not notice them perhaps because they were already openly rewarded by men.

Did you also notice that when Jesus was talking to His disciple about prayer, He instructed them to go into their room, but never when He spoke about fasting?

> *5 "And when you pray, you shall not be like the hypocrites. For they love to pray standing in the synagogues and on the corners of the streets, that they may be seen by men. Assuredly, I say to you, they have their reward. 6 But you, when you pray, go into your room, and when you have shut your door, pray to your Father who is in the secret place; and your Father*

Chapter 9 – Acceptable Fast

who sees in secret will reward you openly" (Matthew 6:5-6).

When you fast, you can go out but when you pray during the fast, go into a room to pray. No one should notice when you fast, but you cannot pray in public without being noticed or without drawing undue attention to self. So we are admonished to seek a quiet place to pray.

God reiterated the characteristics of acceptable fast as conditional to rewarding a fast. Before we turn to the rewards or benefits of fasting, let us briefly see in the later verses of Isaiah 58, the emphasis God placed on the characteristics of the acceptable fast conditional to the blessings of the same.

"9b If you take away the yoke from your midst, the pointing of the finger, and speaking wickedness, 10a If you extend your soul to the hungry, and satisfy the afflicted soul" (Isaiah 58:9b-10a).

Here again, in the later verses, we have a few of the characteristics of the acceptable fast repeated,

- Taking away the yoke from your midst
- Taking away the pointing of the finger

THE FAST TRACK

- Taking away speaking wickedness
- Extending our soul to the hungry
- Satisfying the afflicted soul

Please pray like this for fasting the wrong way.

> *"Almighty and most merciful Father, we have erred and strayed from thy ways, like lost sheep. We have followed too much the devices and desires of our own hearts. We have offended against thy holy laws. We have left undone those things which we ought to have done, and we have done those things which we ought not to have done, and there is no health in us. But thou, O Lord, have mercy upon us miserable offenders. Spare thou them, O God, which confess their faults. Restore thou them that be penitent, according to thy promises declared unto mankind, in Christ Jesus our Lord. And grant, O most merciful Father, for his sake, that we may hereafter live a godly, righteous, and sober life, to the glory of thy holy name" (A General Confession of Sin," from the 1559 edition of Book of Common Prayer.*

Chapter 9 – Acceptable Fast

HONOURING THE SABBATH

> *"If you turn away your foot from the Sabbath, from doing your pleasure on My holy day, and call the Sabbath a delight, the holy day of the Lord honorable, and shall honor Him, not doing your own ways, nor finding your own pleasure, nor speaking your own words"* (Isaiah 58:13).

If someone claims to be righteous and godly, yet ignores the command of the Lord to keep and reverence the Sabbath, such person may fast but not be noticed by the Lord of the Sabbath. The Jews of Isaiah's day did all sorts of things on the Sabbath, fulfilling their natural pleasure, doing their own ways and speaking their own words. Obviously, they were seeking God every day (including Sabbath), yet Sabbath was not treated as a 'Holy Day' and certainly was not taken as a 'Sabbath of Delight.' They did not honour God on the day.

If you dishonour the Sabbath, you dishonour the Lord of The Sabbath. This fits in impeccably with the fulfilment of the Sabbath in light of the completed work of Jesus. When we set aside every day to honour God, we keep the Sabbath.

Moreover, Christians are not required to keep the Sabbath today. The New Testament makes it clear that Christians are not under obligation to observe a Sabbath day because Jesus fulfils the purpose and plan of the Sabbath for us and in us. The rest we enter into as Christians is something to experience every day, not just one day a week. The scriptures tell us that Christians are not bound to observe days and months and seasons and years (Colossians 2:16-17; Galatians 4:9-11; Hebrews 4:9-11).

However, though we are free from the legal obligation of the Sabbath, we dare not ignore the importance of a day of rest - God has built us so that we need one.

Chapter 10

BENEFITS OF ACCEPTABLE FAST

Thus far we have looked at the fast God does not want and the fast chosen by Him. Let us now see the benefits of the second. There are numerous rewards to fasting, but we will only concentrate on those highlighted in Isaiah 58, a chapter upon which we have spent incredible time.

If God's people would couple their fasting with lives of righteousness and love, then they would see more of their prayers answered.

> *"Then your light shall break forth like the morning, your healing shall spring forth speedily, and your righteousness shall go before you; the glory of the LORD shall be your rear guard. Then you shall call, and the LORD will answer; you shall cry, and*

He will say, "Here I am." If you take away the yoke from your midst, the pointing of the finger, and speaking wickedness, if you extend your soul to the hungry and satisfy the afflicted soul, then your light shall dawn in the darkness, and your darkness shall be as the noonday. The LORD will guide you continually, and satisfy your soul in drought, and strengthen your bones; you shall be like a watered garden, and like a spring of water, whose waters do not fail. Those from among you shall build the old waste places; You shall raise up the foundations of many generations; and you shall be called the Repairer of the Breach, the Restorer of Streets to Dwell In" (Isaiah 58:8-12).

YOUR LIGHT SHALL BREAK FORTH LIKE THE MORNING

Morning light is like new unpolluted, unhindered bright light that wakes us up from the restless night. The breaking forth means nothing shall be able to hinder our light. It shall be uncovered and unstoppable.

Chapter 10 – Benefits of Acceptable Fast

YOUR HEALING SHALL SPRING FORTH SPEEDILY

Can you imagine a spring? It is the purest form of water and usually flows slowly. Here God says that your healing will burst forth. There is going to be a quick turnaround in your health. It shall be speedy. Before you have the time to treat any wound, illness or infirmity, it shall be no more.

YOUR RIGHTEOUSNESS SHALL GO BEFORE YOU

Before now, you might have been making your case and demanding your right based on self righteousness. From now, your right standing with God shall be noticed by all. Your fame will be known beyond your borders, and people shall serve you even before they meet you.

THE GLORY OF THE LORD SHALL BE YOUR REAR GUARD

As your righteousness goes before you, so shall God's glory back you up. You will never be afraid of what lies hidden behind you. When people see your back, they shall see the glory of the LORD. What is the glory doing behind you? It is guarding you so that no evil or ill-will can touch you wherever you cannot see or defend yourself.

> *"Then you shall call, and the LORD will answer; you shall cry, and He will say, 'Here I am'"*

This is a two-in-one promise - God will answer you, and will appear to you in His glory. The ears of the Lord will be attentive to your call. Heaven will acknowledge your quest. God promises you His undivided attention. "Here I Am" usually is said by servants. God will never become your servant but dispatch His angels, and they will run to you with the saying "Here I Am."

THEN YOUR LIGHT SHALL DAWN IN THE DARKNESS, AND YOUR DARKNESS SHALL BE AS THE NOONDAY

To those that fast the right way, God promises heavenly blessings. Not only will they partake in pure, unadulterated light just as in the breaking of dawn, but even their darkness shall also be turned to noonday. They will never know

Chapter 10 – Benefits of Acceptable Fast

darkness anymore, never. Their life is an enlightened life.

THE LORD WILL GUIDE YOU CONTINUALLY

It is one thing to enjoy the presence of the Lord and be guided by Him occasionally, but to become a recipient of a continued guidance should be the ultimate desire of all His children. That is the promise to those that observe the Acceptable Fast. Their life is a guided life.

TO SATISFY YOUR SOUL IN DROUGHT, AND STRENGTHEN YOUR BONES

Those who fast with pure hearts and corresponding actions shall enjoy perfect health and never suffer lack. They live a life of satisfaction, and abundant blessing of the soul. The strengthening of the bones means they will be far from being feeble. They will always be strong and agile. Their life is a happy life.

YOU SHALL BE LIKE A WATERED GARDEN

A watered garden is a garden that is always fresh, green and lush. Thus, a life like a watered garden will always remain fresh and flourishing. Their life is a fragrantly green life.

THE FAST TRACK

YOU SHALL BE LIKE A SPRING OF WATER, WHOSE WATERS DO NOT FAIL

Like a spring of water, such life will always be fruitful in all seasons. They will remain relevant throughout the year. Their life is a freshly sustained life.

Those from among you shall build the old waste places; You shall raise up the foundations of many generations; and you shall be called the Repairer of the Breach, the Restorer of Streets to Dwell In.

Those who fast with pure hearts and corresponding actions also get things done for the kingdom of God. They are kingdom builders. They are very original and great pioneers. They fix cracks and are good renovators of run-down lives. They put things back together for the benefit of those alive and those unborn. Their life is a productive, healing life.

Finally, we discover more benefits of the Acceptable Fast from the last two verses of Isaiah 58.

> *"If you turn away your foot from the Sabbath, from doing your pleasure on My holy day, and call the Sabbath a delight, the holy day of the LORD honorable, and*

Chapter 10 – Benefits of Acceptable Fast

shall honor Him, not doing your own ways, nor finding your own pleasure, nor speaking your own words, then you shall delight yourself in the LORD; and I will cause you to ride on the high hills of the earth, and feed you with the heritage of Jacob your father. The mouth of the LORD has spoken."

As if it were an addendum to the chapter on fasting, we see more benefits when the Sabbath observance is restored especially during the fast period. When we keep the significance of the Sabbath, not simply as an empty religious ritual,

- We shall delight ourselves in the LORD. God will pour out His blessing upon us, and we shall delight in the LORD Himself, not only in the blessings.
- He will cause us to ride on the high hills of the earth
- We will be fed with Jacob's heritage
- We know it shall happen because the mouth of the LORD has spoken.

THE FAST TRACK

CHAPTER 11

THE DANIEL FAST

Let us now take a closer look at Daniel chapter ten for insight on Daniel Fast.

1 "In the third year of the reign of King Cyrus of Persia, Daniel (also known as Belteshazzar) had another vision. He understood that the vision concerned events certain to happen in the future — times of war and great hardship. 2 When this vision came to me, I, Daniel, had been in mourning for three whole weeks. 3 All that time I had eaten no rich food. No meat or wine crossed my lips, and I used no fragrant lotions until those three weeks had passed."

THE FAST TRACK

A UNIQUE EXPERIENCE

Daniel fasted for 21 days, but it was not a 21-day Daniel Fast as many have suggested. After some had returned with Ezra from exile at the decree of Cyprus for their restoration, Daniel purposed to fast for the brethren, the Jews; to ask God for mercy and to seek God's mind regarding their future.

Daniel was praying for as long as it would take to receive a favourable answer from heaven. When he prayed, his request was granted from the first day, though he had no revelation of such. So, he carried on praying. Daniel would have stopped praying and fasting if the reply to his request were received the same day. There would not have been any further need for him to have carried on.

In the same way, Daniel would have carried on with fasting as he was determined to, for as long as it would have taken had he not received the answer to his request on the 21st day.

In effect, the Daniel Fast is not a fast for 21 days but a fast for as long as it takes to receive an answer. Anyone engaged in the Daniel Fast should be prepared to go as long as it might take to receive a favourable answer. This can be longer or shorter than 21 days.

Chapter 11 – The Daniel Fast

Daniel Fast is unique in some ways.

It is the only fast of its kind. There is no other 21-day fast in the whole of scripture. There are numerous 40-day, 3-day and 1-day fasts in the Bible but only a mention of 21-day fast.

It is also unique in that it was the only fast that took heaven (and earth) by storm. And what do I mean by that? Heaven was literally empty of Archangels during this fast. Remember, of the three Archangels, Lucifer was already demoted to earth but the remaining two Archangels, Gabriel and Michael were dispatched for this particular mission.

Also, the Daniel Fast was a partial fast. Some people call it white fast. I have no idea where that came from. What I know is that the Daniel Fast (Daniel now aged, possibly 84), was not a total abstention from eating or drinking; it was a fast avoiding pastries, meat and wine and Daniel must have eaten unpalatable bread and drank some water.

Finally, Daniel Fast was a fast for understanding. Although Daniel got more than he bargained for in this fast, his primary reason for fasting was to get the mind of God and to gain understanding (verses 1, 12 & 14). Some fasts in the Bible had dual or multipurpose agenda to them. Others had singular agenda, yet they are entirely different to Daniel Fast.

What then should we expect from Daniel Fast?

PERSONAL, DIVINE REVELATION

You are about to receive a personal, private word from God. In the midst of noises and the crowd, you are going to hear from God so clearly and so distinctly, and the word you hear will be personal.

> *7 "Only I, Daniel, saw this vision. The men with me saw nothing, but they were suddenly terrified and ran away to hide. 8 So I was left there all alone to see this amazing vision. My strength left me, my face grew deathly pale, and I felt very weak. 9 Then I heard the man speak, and when I heard the sound of his voice, I fainted and lay there with my face to the ground. 21 Meanwhile, I will tell you what is written in the Book of Truth. (No one helps me against these spirit princes except Michael, your spirit prince."*

Chapter 11 – The Daniel Fast

A TOUCH FROM HEAVEN

Everyone desiring a touch from heaven gets one during this fast. Daniel had a touch from heaven to allay his fears. Yours may be for healing, deliverance or breakthrough in the area of your marriage, money or ministry.

> *10 "Just then a hand touched me and lifted me, still trembling, to my hands and knees. 11 And the man said to me, "Daniel, you are very precious to God, so listen carefully to what I have to say to you. Stand up, for I have been sent to you." When he said this to me, I stood up, still trembling. 12 Then he said, "Don't be afraid, Daniel. Since the first day you began to pray for understanding and to humble yourself before your God, your request has been heard in heaven. I have come in answer to your prayer."*

HEAVEN'S ATTENTION

Daniel Fast was one that provoked heaven's attention. Daniel was unaware that he was noticed right from the first day he began to seek God's face, but we do. His prayers were heard from the very first day. From now on, your prayers will be heard and acknowledged.

> *12 Then he said, "Don't be afraid, Daniel. Since the first day you began to pray for understanding and to humble yourself before your God, your request has been heard in heaven. I have come in answer to your prayer."*

HEAVENLY REINFORCEMENT

This is the end to every delay in your life. For your sakes, God is going to send help from heaven in the person of the 'Warring Angel' named Michael to release the rest of your blessings.

> *13 "But for twenty-one days the spirit prince of the kingdom of Persia blocked my way. Then Michael, one of the archangels, came to help me, and I left him there with the spirit prince of the kingdom of Persia. 21 Meanwhile, I will tell you what is written in the Book of Truth. (No one helps me against these spirit princes except Michael, your spirit prince."*

Chapter 11 – The Daniel Fast

ANGELIC VISITATION

Twice, Daniel received the assurance of an angelic visitation. Before this, all he experienced was a vision (vs. 5-9). For everyone who would take part in this Daniel Fast, get ready for a visitation by the 'Blessing/Messenger Angel' named Gabriel. You are due for more good tidings.

> *12 "Then he said, "Don't be afraid, Daniel. Since the first day you began to pray for understanding and to humble yourself before your God, your request has been heard in heaven. I have come in answer to your prayer. 14 Now I am here to explain what will happen to your people in the future, for this vision concerns a time yet to come."*

PROPHETIC INSIGHT

God wants us to get ahead of many future uncertainties by revealing them during this fast. You are going to receive prophetic insights into 'what will happen to your people in the latter days.' God is about to reveal His blueprint for 'many days yet to come' concerning your job, ministry, and this nation especially.

14 "Now I am here to explain what will happen to your people in the future, for this vision concerns a time yet to come."

PEACE OF MIND & RENEWED STRENGTH

Peace, calm, tranquillity and serenity are parts to the complete package. There is no point having prophecy and prosperity without peace. Above all, your strength will be renewed. New vigour and new hope will come in place of weariness and discouragement.

15 "While he was speaking to me, I looked down at the ground, unable to say a word. 16 Then the one who looked like a man[f] touched my lips, and I opened my mouth and began to speak. I said to the one standing in front of me, "I am filled with anguish because of the vision I have seen, my lord, and I am very weak. 17 How can someone like me, your servant, talk to you, my lord? My strength is gone, and I can hardly breathe." 18 Then the one who looked like a man touched me again, and I felt my strength returning. 19 "Don't be afraid," he said, "for you are very

Chapter 11 – The Daniel Fast

precious to God. Peace! Be encouraged! Be strong!"

DANIEL FAST TIPS

- Go as long as it will take to receive an answer. Do not break it in the middle even if you can only fast part of each day.
- The Daniel Fast is a sober fast. He ate nothing desirable – just something to keep him going (no meat and no wine, verse 3). This is what it means: Do not strive to eat two meals between 6pm and 12midnight or go partying at the weekend. You must be consistent throughout the entire period of your fast. Do not take weekend breaks.
- The Daniel Fast is a humbling fast (verse 12). No points can be won for fasting when other people are unable. You do not suddenly become more spiritual because you fast. So please do it in an attitude of humility.
- Keep confessing God's word. This is what the angels act on (Psalms 103:20). Daniel said "… while I was speaking in prayer …" (Daniel 9:21), and the angel

said "…, your words were heard; and I have come because of your words" (Daniel 10:12).
- Pray before breaking each day.
- A normal Jewish fast is from dusk to dusk but you should endeavour to fast from 12 midnight until 6pm daily.
- If you are pregnant or on any form of medication, seek medical advice, but pray.

CHAPTER 12

WHY ALL MAJOR RELIGION FAST

The purpose of this chapter is to highlight the need for fasting. If anything can be learnt from other religion, it is the fact that they recognise the importance of fasting. I am not suggesting in any way that the religion is acceptable, or that their fast or the reasons they fast is agreeable; I am only stating that there must be something good and valuable about fasting that makes all religion to want to fast.

I have listed the major religion in alphabetical order and not in the other of the importance or purpose of their fasts.

BAHÁ'Í

The Bahá'í Faith was founded by Bahá'u'lláh in 19th-century Persia. The Baha'i fast usually take place during the 19th day of the Bahá'í year, called Ala, which is from the second to the twentieth day of March. From sunrise to sunset, Baha'is abstain from food and drinks. The Bahá'í fast so as to give devotion to their God and also to matters of spiritual nature.

BUDDHIST

From the Tendai to the Tibetan, to the Theravadin, and to all the major branches of Buddhism, part of the year is set aside to observe some form of fasting. This usually takes place on some holidays and full-moon days. For the Buddhist, though some liquids are permitted, abstention from solid food is a must depending on the tradition. For most, fasting is a method of purifying the person. For example, the Tibetan monks fast as a way of aiding feats in yoga called yogic feats. Here, such practices generate internal heat. However, the Tendai and Theravadin monks fast so as to free their minds.

CATHOLIC

It is well known that when the Catholics fast, they abstain from meat on two Holy days; Ash Wednesday and Good Friday. Also, they refrain from meat on all Fridays in the entire 40 days of

Chapter 12 – Why All Major Religion Fast

Lent. Before the 1960s, it is forbidden for a Catholic to eat meat on any Friday but since the mid-1960s, local discretion may permit a Catholic to eat meat on Fridays other than those during the Lenten period.

Two small and one regular meal are allowed on Ash Wednesday and Good Friday but eating meat is forbidden. For some people with medical condition, pregnant women, and others with reasonable excuses, the Friday fast can be optional. Instead of fasting, they can substitute a different penance or observe special prayers.

For the Catholic, the purpose of fasting is either to control fleshly desires, observe solidarity with the poor or to make penance for their sins. By practicing austerity, fasting prepares the soul for a greater feast. On Good Friday, fasting is considered commemoratory of the suffering of Christ.

EASTERN ORTHODOX

Apart from the Lenten fast, the Eastern Orthodox observe several fast periods during the year. These include Nativity Dormition Fast, Apostles' Fast and several one-day fasts. Except weeks designated as fast-free weeks, two days of the week are set aside to fast. These are Wednesdays and Fridays.

Meat, dairy products, and eggs are not allowed during these fasting days whereas fish are prohibited on some fast days and allowed on others.

Amongst other reasons, the Eastern Orthodox fast to strengthen their resistance to gluttony and also open themselves to God's grace.

HINDU

The Hindu fast is popularly observed during the festive seasons of Saraswati Puja, Shivaratri, Durga Puja (sometimes called Navaratri), and on New Moon days, and other festivals. On the day of Karva Chauth, some women in North of India also fast.

There are no set rules as for the time of the day or the duration in hours as to the Hindu fast. Depending on the individual, the fasting may include a 24-hour period of total abstention from any food or drink (or both), but it is more often the non-eating of solid foods, the drinking of water, or milk occasionally.

Sometimes regarded as a sacrifice, fasting for the Hindu is a means of enhancing their focus during a period of meditation and worship.

Chapter 12 – Why All Major Religion Fast

Likewise, it is also a means of purification for the body system.

JEWISH

In the Jewish year calendar, there are about eight major Jewish fasts; six general ones, Yom Kippur (also known as the Day of Atonement), and the Tisha B'Av (also noted as the day on which the destruction of the Jewish Temple took place). Yom Kippur is the Jewish best-known fast day

When the Jews fast on the Day of Atonement (Yom Kippur) and on the day on which the temple was destroyed (Tisha B'Av), it usually takes up to twenty-five hours, from sundown to sundown and no food or drink can be taken during the fast. However, on the other six fast days, and depending on the season of the year, no food or drink is allowed from sunrise to sundown only.

All Jewish fasts so their sins may be atoned for and to bring before God, their special needs and requests.

THE FAST TRACK

MORMON

From time immemorial, Mormon fast every first Sunday of the month abstaining from drinks and food missing out two meals during the day. They also donate their food and give financial support to the needy. After that, a "fast or testimonial meeting" is held by the members of the church to end the fast. At will, individuals, families, or wards may observe other fasts during the month.

The significance of the Mormon fast is to draw closer to God and to be able to concentrate on God and religion. Also, when the individual, families or wards fasts, it may be done to petition God for something specific, like healing for a sick person or to seek God's face for making a difficult decision.

MUSLIM

Historically, the ninth month of the Islam's lunar calendar is regarded as the month when the Qur'an was first revealed to Prophet Mohammad. Ever since, Ramadan, the Muslim Fast, became mandatory during this period. In addition to this month-long season of fasting,

Chapter 12 – Why All Major Religion Fast

other days and periods of tastings are recommended by various Muslim customs.

The Ramadan fast require abstinence from smoking, food, sexual intercourse, drink, and profane language from before the break of dawn until sunset for the entire month.

Though there is a slight disagreement as to whether it is on a Monday or a Thursday that prophet Mohammad fasted, it is agreed that he fasted once every week. So you may find some Muslims fasting every Monday while others fast every Thursday. Other Muslims fast during the three days leading to Ramadan or during the month of Sha'baan which comes before Ramadan.

Fasting during Ramadan is one of the five pillars of Islam – the five key practices that underpin the Islamic faith. Muslims believe that the physical ritual allows them to understand the suffering of others as well as increasing their closeness to God. The fast of Ramadan is a time for patience, endurance, reflection and spiritual purification.

PAGAN

Pagans are those holding religious beliefs other than those of the main world religions.

With the pagans, there are no organised fast days. However, in readiness for the Spring Equinox (also known as Ostara), some pagans may choose to fast.

When they fast, some of them fully abstain from taking any food while others just reduce the amount of their food intake. This is done entirely at the discretion of the person fasting.

The reason why the pagans fast is to purify the person energetically, thereby raising their vibrational levels as they prepare for magical work. The Ostara fast is used to cleanse the individual from heavier winter foods.

PROTESTANT (EVANGELICAL)

Evangelical Protestants do not force members or organisations to a set period of fasting. Fasting is done at the discretion of individuals, organisations, churches, or communities.

Fasting varies from total abstinence from food or drink to drinking just water or juice, to eating only certain foods or skipping certain meals, or by abstaining from temptations, whether or not edible.

In recent times, Evangelical fasts have grown in popularity. Today, people fast for just about everything including for spiritual nourishment, being in solidarity with victims of poverty, or fasting just to serve as a counterbalance to modern consumer culture, or to petition God for special needs.

PROTESTANT (MAINLINE)

Fasting for the Mainline Protestant does not form a major part of their tradition. Therefore fasts can be held at the sole discretion of individuals, communities, churches, and other groups. Whatever happens during such fast lay at the discretion of the person or people fasting.

Mainline fasting is mainly to improve their spiritual standing or to advance a political or social justice cause. An example of Mainline Protestant fast is the ELCA's "Campaign of Prayer, Fasting, and Vigils."

THE FAST TRACK

CHAPTER 13

FASTING PRAYER POINTS WITH SCRIPTURES

These set of prayers may guide you along as you wait on the Lord. They may be used alongside any other prayer book. They are not arranged in particular order. Please read and meditate on the words and the Lord will bless your time in Jesus Christ name. Amen.

- Give thanks unto the Lord for His goodness concerning your job, family, relationships, church, leaders, etc. (Psalms 100; 1 Thessalonians 5:16-19).
- Pray for the government especially for the leader (president or prime minister) and all the members of the government including your elected House members (1 Timothy 2:1-2; Ezekiel 22:1-End).

- Pray that God will bless the royal family and they will reflect the heavenly royalty. Pray also for all their children as well (1 Timothy 2:1-4 & 2 Corinthians 4:3-4).
- Pray for the peace of Jerusalem, Palestine, and Israel. Pray also for your city against any terrorist attacks, against the principalities of homosexual, drugs, and violence (Psalms 122:1-End).
- Pray for the salvation of your family and relatives. Thank God for saving you and calling you His son/daughter (Acts 10:1-35 & 2 Peter 3:9).
- Pray for the salvation of those who are related to you: friend, employer, employees, neighbours, teachers, students, etc. Pray that God will open their eyes (Acts 10:36-48 & 1 Timothy 1:15-16).
- Pray for your spiritual leaders and those who keep watch over your soul by name. Pray that God will continue to supply their needs and keep their families (1 Thessalonians 2:12-13 & 1 Timothy 5:17).

Chapter 13 – Fasting Prayer Points with Scriptures

- Like Moses, much of the weight of spiritual leadership lies on your pastor. So please lift him/her up before God; and the wife/husband also (Ephesians 6:19).
- Pray that God will bless the ministry of the leaders and grant them the spirit of wisdom and understanding in His word and that His power in them will be beyond measure (Matthew 26:31 & 1 Thessalonians 2:12-13).
- Pray for the ministries in the Church that God will send labourers into the vineyard. If you have not been involved in any department, pray that God will give you direction (Matthew 9:37-38).
- Pray that God will raise up Timothys, Tituss, and Joshuas for the work of the ministry. People who are faithful, loyal and dedicated to God's work (Luke 10:1-12 & 2 Timothy 2:2).
- Pray that the AGAPE love of God will permeate every facet of our ministries and meetings (1 Corinthians 13:1-End).
- Pray that God will open up more areas of ministry in your Church to those

who have gifts that are not yet recognised so they can fulfil their ministries (Colossians 3:16 & Ephesians 5:19).

- Pray that God will open more doors of ministry and Church plants both locally and internationally (Colossians 4:3 & Psalms 2:8).
- Pray for all the new Churches and their pastors; for strength and courage. Pray also for new ones that will be started in the future for God to direct the leaders (Matthew 28:19-20 & Mark 16:15-18).
- Pray for your spiritual growth that you may have a better relationship with God and that He may find you a better tool for His service (1 Peter 2:2-3 & Philippians 3:1-End).
- Pray that you will not fall into temptation; that Jesus who has been through all temptations without sinning will be there for you (1 Corinthians 10:12-13 & Hebrews 4:15-16).
- Pray that the peace of God will rule and reign in our families: husbands loving their wives, wives submitting to

Chapter 13 – Fasting Prayer Points with Scriptures

their husbands and children obeying their parents (1 Peter 3:1-12).

- Of all that God made there is one thing that is not good – "that man should be alone." Pray for singles that they will meet their partners (Ecclesiastes 4:9-12 & Genesis 2:18-25).
- Pray for the children; for knowledge, wisdom, protection, etc. even as their angels behold the face of God (Matthew 18:1-11).
- If there had been dreams that seem to be dead, aspirations almost forgotten, pray for their resurrection and restoration in the name of Jesus (Ezekiel 37:1-End).
- Pray that whatever the enemy has stolen from you will be restored back seven fold. Pray also for restoration of all the Church had lost (Joel 2:1-End).
- Pray for the unity in the body of Christ in the whole world and in your country of residence. More can be achieved if we are one (John 17:1-End & Psalms 133:1-End).
- If someone you know has an immigration problem, pray that this

shall be his or her time of deliverance. Pray for open doors for married couples not living together in the same country (Isaiah 52:1-End & Psalms 18:18).

- Pray that as the Church of God grows spiritually, she will also grow numerically in regular attendants (Acts 2:47 & Acts 6:7).
- Pray for all pregnant women in the Church at large against miscarriages and that the face of the Lord will shine upon those trusting Him for Children (Psalms 113:1-End & Exodus 23:26).
- If you belong to any group in the church, pray for all its members by name mentioning specific areas of needs (1 Samuel 12:22-25 & Galatians 4:19).
- God's promise to you is that "no plague shall come near your dwelling." Claim this for yourself, and if you are sick, "by His stripes ye were healed," past tense (1 Peter 2:24 & Psalms 91:10).
- Pray for anyone you know that is sick, be it your neighbour, friend, relative or a member of your family that God

Chapter 13 – Fasting Prayer Points with Scriptures

should touch their infirmities (James 5:16 & Psalms 107:20).

- Plead the blood of Jesus over all that belongs to you against any sudden death and also for the Church against any loss of lives (Exodus 12:1-End & Psalms 118:17).
- Pray for the men and women ministries in your church towards achieving their aim and objectives (Acts 13:1-4).
- Pray for God's supernatural financial abundance until there will be no more room to contain it as you faithfully tithe and give an offering (2 Corinthians 9:8 & Psalms 23:1-End).
- Pray that people without jobs will meet with God's favour. Pray also that God will protect the jobs; no problems, only promotion (Ephesians 4:28 & Psalms 28:1-End).
- If you are trusting God to start a business, pray for guidance to make the right choices. If you are already in business, pray for fruitfulness in all your endeavours (Psalms 1:1-End).

- Pray for material blessings; new cars, new homes, new jobs, etc. Pray also for all material needs of your pastor calling them by name (Philippians 4:19 & 3 John 2).
- Pray that God will grant you church favour on your building projects. Pray that God will stir up people's heart towards giving (Exodus 35:1-End).
- If you need strength to walk with God, all you need is the joy of the Lord. He will turn your mourning into dancing. Pray that you will receive joy in place of past grief (Nehemiah 8:1-12).
- Pray that God will keep and sustain you while you wait to receive the physical manifestation of what you have prayed for (Psalms 40:1-End).
- Always submit the prayer requests under God's will so you can have His blessings without any sorrow (Matthew 26:30-39 & I John 5:14-15).
- Only prayers offered with a thankful heart gets the desired results. If you want the desired results, there is nothing else to do than to start praising God for your miracles (Philippians 4:6).

Other Books by Sam O. Adewunmi

- 31 Words that will Change your life Forever
- Good Finish to Bad Start
- Your Basket, Kneading Bowl and Barn
- Turning Temptations into Triumphs
- Healed, in Jesus' Name

www.ingramcontent.com/pod-product-compliance
Lightning Source LLC
Chambersburg PA
CBHW061947070426
42450CB00007BA/1079